The York Princesses

The daughters of Edward IV and Elizabeth Woodville

Also by Sarah J Hodder

The Queen's Sisters – The Lives of the Sisters of
Elizabeth Woodville

The York Princesses

The daughters of Edward IV and Elizabeth Woodville

Sarah J. Hodder

Winchester, UK
Washington, USA

JOHN HUNT PUBLISHING

First published by Chronos Books, 2021
Chronos Books is an imprint of John Hunt Publishing Ltd., No. 3 East St., Alresford,
Hampshire SO24 9EE, UK
office@jhpbooks.com
www.johnhuntpublishing.com
www.chronosbooks.com

For distributor details and how to order please visit the 'Ordering' section on our website.

Text copyright: Sarah J. Hodder 2020

ISBN: 978 1 78904 557 4
978 1 78904 558 1 (ebook)
Library of Congress Control Number: 2020933341

A CIP catalogue record for this book is available from the British Library.

Design: Stuart Davies

UK: Printed and bound by CPI Group (UK) Ltd, Croydon, CR0 4YY
Printed in North America by CPI GPS partners

We operate a distinctive and ethical publishing philosophy in
all areas of our business, from our global network of authors to
production and worldwide distribution.

Contents

Introduction   1

Edward IV's First Reign: In a Nutshell   6

Chapter One: Elizabeth of York, 1466 - 1503   14

Chapter Two: Mary of York, 1467-1482   45

Chapter Three: Cecily of York, 1469-1507   51

Chapter Four: Margaret of York, 1472   67

Chapter Five: Anne of York, 1475-1511   77

Chapter Six: Katherine of York, 1479-1527   97

Chapter Seven: Bridget of York, 1480-1507   119

The End of an Era   130

References   133

Select Bibliography   143

Introduction

The marriage of King Edward IV to Elizabeth Woodville was highly controversial even from its humble beginnings in a hermitage in the sleepy Northamptonshire village of Grafton Regis. A beautiful widow with two young sons, Elizabeth was considered a commoner, and a highly unsuitable match for the Yorkist King. She and her Woodville relations were unpopular with many of the great and noble families in the country who resented their steep and sudden ascent to power that resulted from her marriage. Labelled upstarts and social climbers, it is a reputation that is still attributed to them even today. Her father, Richard Woodville, was a mere soldier who had served in France under the Duke of Bedford. The fact that through her mother's side she was descended from one of the most distinguished families in Luxembourg, the Counts of Saint Pol, and that her mother, Jacquetta, had once been married to the very same Duke of Bedford that her second husband had served, making her, at one point, one of the highest ranking Ladies in England, was overlooked by those wishing to disparage her.

On 1st May 1464, Elizabeth Woodville made what many deemed a fortuitous marriage to the Yorkist King of England, Edward IV, although for Elizabeth and Edward it was simply a love match. They made their vows in secret, at her home, with only Elizabeth's mother taken into their confidence. The marriage was not revealed publicly for almost four months, until during a council meeting at Reading in September that year, Edward had been questioned on his choice of future bride and had revealed that the discussions were unnecessary, he was in fact already married. In later years it would be said that Elizabeth had enchanted him into marrying her and she would be accused, albeit not formally, of witchcraft. Her mother would also have to officially defend herself against accusations of sorcery and enchantment.

But despite their detractors, Edward and Elizabeth were married for eighteen years. Having only ascended to the throne himself in 1461, deposing the old King, Henry VI, by defeating him and the Lancastrian army on the battlefield at Towton, Elizabeth was by his side for the majority of his twenty-one-year reign.

During their marriage they had ten children together. Three of these were boys of whom one, George Duke of Bedford, did not survive past the age of two, dying in 1479. Their other two sons, Edward, Prince of Wales, and Richard, Duke of York, would grow up and become known to history as the ill-fated Princes in the Tower. Their story is still one of the great unsolved mysteries; their disappearance from the Tower where they were housed after the death of their father whilst awaiting Edward's coronation as Edward V, remains unexplained to this day. The usurpation of the throne by their uncle Richard, Duke of Gloucester, who went on to become Richard III, led many of his contemporaries and historians across the subsequent centuries to suspect that he had a hand in their disappearance. No definitive proof survives of his involvement and convincing arguments have been made asserting his innocence and apportioning the blame in the direction of others, including Elizabeth's brother-in-law and close associate of Richard, the Duke of Buckingham, and Margaret Beaufort, the mother of the future King Henry VII. Pretenders at the later Tudor Court would insist they were the lost Princes, with one of them, known to history as Perkin Warbeck, presenting a highly convincing case that perhaps one of the two Princes of York did manage to escape their imprisonment. The fate of the two boys may now never truly be discovered, although bones found in 1674 by workmen at the Tower of London, digging below the stairs that led from the Royal Apartments to the White Tower are purported to belong to two young boys. The bones were reburied in Westminster Abbey by Charles II. Further DNA testing has not yet been allowed and may never be.

As well as George, Richard and Edward, the King and Queen were also parents to seven girls. It wouldn't be unmerited to say that most of the York Princesses fared better in their lives than their unfortunate brothers did, although Thomas More writing in his history of Richard III laments that 'the division and dissension of their friends' had unarmed them and left them destitute'. Certainly, during their early years, all the royal siblings led a charmed existence, adored by their parents and safely ensconced within court life. Three of the oldest girls, Elizabeth, Mary and Cecily, had been born and would have been caught up in the tumultuous period of 1470-71, when their father was forced to flee abroad, and their mother took sanctuary in Westminster Abbey, fearing for her life, but at this point the girls would have been only four, three and one year respectively, so it is likely that only the eldest Elizabeth, if any, would have had memories of this time.

Describing Christmas at court in 1482, the writer of the Croyland Chronicle remarks that the royal court presented an appearance that 'fully befits a most mighty kingdom, filled with riches and boasting of those sweet and beautiful children, the issue of his marriage with Queen Elizabeth'. Certainly, the young princesses and their brothers at this point in their childhood would have been thriving, feeling safe and secure within the royal family and sure of their destinies. For Edward Prince of Wales, he was being raised as the future King of England, his brother Richard his loyal supporter, who would perhaps follow in the footsteps of his uncle, Richard, and become a powerful magnate in the north, assisting Edward in ruling the Kingdom. For the young princesses, their future was not to rule England, but to attain suitable marriages, ideally to Princes of other Kingdoms where they would rule alongside their husbands or at the very least to one of the noble men of the realm.

But then in 1483 fortune's wheel turned, as it is liable to do, and in April of that year the sudden and unexpected death of their father ended life as they knew it. What should have inevitably been a sad occasion followed by a time of celebration as their elder brother rightly took his place on the throne of England, turned into what could arguably be described as the worst moments of their young lives. Under threat from their uncle, Richard, and with their family thrown into turmoil, they were forced to flee into sanctuary with their mother – the second time Elizabeth Woodville had had to run with her children into the safety of Westminster Abbey.

From 1483 onwards, the York princesses had to adjust to a different way of life, initially having to come to terms with the deaths of their father and the subsequent disappearance of their brothers as well as their new bleak living surroundings, confined as they were to lodgings within the Abbey. As time passed and the dust began to settle, they were then required to navigate the new court of their uncle, Richard III, having to adjust to new and unexpected futures that would have been completely different to what had been planned for them as royal children.

With the exception, perhaps, of Elizabeth of York, who was the eldest York girl and who went on to marry Henry Tudor to become the first Queen of the Tudor age, the lives of the remaining daughters of Edward and Elizabeth fade into the annals of history. But these women grew up, lived and even thrived into the Tudor years, marrying, having children and bearing witness to other events that happened that we read about in our history books today.

This book is a brief discussion of each of their lives. By necessity, some of the chapters are longer than others, as some of the sisters have left only a brief mark in the historical records. Also, by necessity, the chapter on Elizabeth of York, is shorter than it could be as due to her elevated position as Queen of England, numerous accounts of her life survive and whole books have been dedicated to her. But I hope that using the sparse information we can find on these seven women, I have been able to bring them to life once more and to tell their stories in a way that is deserving of the Princesses of York, women who were close to the throne throughout their lives and who ultimately survived the period known as the Wars of the Roses.

Edward IV's First Reign – In a Nutshell

To appreciate the early lives of the Princesses of York, it is useful to have an understanding of the world that they were born into, the background of events that led to the reign of their father, and the conflicts that occurred during his first reign as King of England, much of which happened before they were born. Edward's first reign began in March 1461 and ran to October 1470, and by the end of this period, his three eldest daughters were mere toddlers. The years 1455 to 1485 are known to us now as 'The Wars of the Roses', as the House of York, symbolised by the White Rose, pitted itself against the House of Lancaster, the Red Rose. Whole books have been written on the period, and the battles, the political intrigue, and not forgetting the human stories from that time, keep historians enthralled as they discuss, debate and dissect the events that occurred, the motives of those involved and the outcomes which shaped the future of the history of England.

The young princesses of York were all born into this era, and their early lives certainly were shaped by the conflict between the House of York and the House of Lancaster.

The ruling house prior to Edward IV's reign had been the House of Lancaster, so called as they descended from the third son of Edward III, John of Gaunt, Duke of Lancaster. On the death of Henry V in 1422, his nine-month-old son ascended the throne of England as Henry VI. A regency council was formed to rule in the King's name until he was old enough to do so himself, headed up by his uncles, John Duke of Bedford, who oversaw the ongoing war in France, and Humphrey Duke of Gloucester, who remained in England to lead the country on behalf of the young King. Incidentally, it was this John, Duke of Bedford, who would marry a seventeen-year-old Jacquetta, daughter of the Count of Saint Pol, and who would go on to become Elizabeth

Woodville's mother in later life.

In 1437 at the age of fifteen, Henry VI took over the reins of Government. Eight years later, he would marry Margaret of Anjou, a niece of the French King, in order to procure a peace with France. Whether the couple were compatible is debatable, but her loyalty was never in doubt; in later years Margaret would fight fiercely in defence of her husband and her throne.

The couple's first child whom they named Edward was born at the end of 1453. Just before she gave birth to her son, however, King Henry VI had mysteriously fallen into a depression or stupor. The royal physicians were at a loss to diagnose his condition, which came on suddenly and rendered him into a coma-like state – awake but completely unresponsive. As such, he was unable to communicate, let alone effectively rule. January 1454 saw Queen Margaret making a case for her to rule in his place until such time that her husband was recovered. She needed to safeguard herself and her new-born son, whom the King had so far not even been able to acknowledge as his own. But England was not yet ready for a female ruler and her case was rejected, the council instead electing to make the Duke of York (Edward IV's father) Protector of the Realm until such time as Henry VI was well again. And so began the Wars of the Roses, or the Cousins War as it was known at the time.

Richard Plantagenet, the Duke of York, also had a claim to the throne of England; he was descended from Edward III, through two lines of descent. His father was the son of Edmund, the 1st Duke of York and fourth son of Edward III, and his mother was a great granddaughter of Lionel, Duke of Clarence, the second of Edward III's sons.

It soon became clear that Henry VI's mental state was not improving, and many began to consider him unfit to rule. From 1454 onwards battle lines were drawn, and the most powerful men in England began to take sides. The Duke of York's most prominent supporter was his nephew, Richard Neville, the Earl of Warwick, an influential magnate and military man. The pair made a formidable team and from 1454 to 1460, they plotted and schemed and fought together against the Lancastrians for the cause they believed in, which was to depose Henry VI in place of the Duke of York.

However, disaster struck in December 1460 when the Duke and his second-born son, Edmund, were killed at the Battle of Wakefield. The Duke's eldest son, Edward, Earl of March, wanted revenge and after a bloody battle on the snow-covered fields of Towton in March 1461, the Yorkists emerged triumphant and Edward was proclaimed Edward IV, King of England. The old King, Henry, was captured and placed in the tower; his wife Margaret and their son Edward fled abroad.

For the first few years of his reign Edward concentrated on establishing himself firmly on the throne with the support of his family and his cousin, friend and advisor, Warwick, the 'Kingmaker'. He was a hugely popular King with the common touch, and as More tells us 'he was a godly personage, and very princely to behold; of heart courageous, politic in counsel; in adversity nothing abashed, in prosperity rather joyful than proud; in peace just and merciful, in war sharp and fierce; in the field bold and hardy, and nevertheless no farther than wisdom would adventurous'.

But in 1464, his marriage to Elizabeth Woodville caused a split between Edward and Warwick, which over time seemed to widen until the chasm became too large to heal. The Earl had created a King, but soon found he couldn't control him.

As the 1460s were coming to an end, the disaffected Earl of Warwick began causing trouble. He and Edward IV had been on a collision course for a while. Edward's next youngest brother George, Duke of Clarence, was also falling under Warwick's influence, causing a rift between the two brothers. Ostensibly handsome and charismatic, and certainly indulged by his older brother, George was also spoilt and easily led. As early as 1467, Warwick had broached the idea of a marriage between George and his eldest daughter, Isabel Neville. Perhaps sensing a collusion between his wayward brother and the powerful Warwick was a dangerous idea, Edward flatly refused to even consider the notion. But then on 11th July 1469, in a direct violation of Edward's ruling, the pair went ahead and married anyway in the port of Calais. But this was no love match. With Edward having not yet borne a son, if they could get him out of the way, (although Warwick may have been unsure at this stage how exactly they were going to make that happen), George would be next in line to be King with Warwick's daughter as his Queen. George, seeing a route to untold riches and power and likely bored of being an underdog to his elder brother, went along with the plan.

The year 1469 had begun with organised uprisings and skirmishes in the north, engineered by Warwick and his men, which Edward was startlingly slow at responding to, perhaps considering them inconsequential at the time. But by the end of June, Edward realised he would have to deal with the troubles, and leaving Elizabeth on progress in Norwich, he and his men headed towards Fotheringhay, issuing a demand for Warwick and Clarence to join him. As he waited for them in Northampton, he had no idea that the pair had left the country for Calais, where they remained for five days to witness the wedding of Isabel and Clarence. After the wedding, Warwick issued what could only be described as a rebel manifesto to Edward, signed by himself, Clarence and Archbishop George Neville, pledging their support to the rebels and accusing members of the Queen's family as well as others around the King of allowing the realm to 'fall in great poverty of misery…. Only intending to their own promotion and enriching'.[1] Clarence and Warwick then returned from France and began marching north with the intention of joining the rebels. By that point, Edward had reached Newark, where he received notification of Warwick and Clarence's treachery. Meanwhile the Earls of Pembroke and Devon who had risen up in support of their King, met up with the rebels on Wednesday 26th July, where in a surprise attack, which later became known as the Battle of Edgecote, the Yorkist forces were routed. In a horrific turn of events for the Woodville family, Earl Rivers and John Woodville, the Queen's father and brother, were captured and beheaded at Kenilworth, on the orders the Duke of Clarence and Earl of Warwick.

For his next move, Warwick made a doomed attempt at taking control of the King. Hearing the news of Edgecote, many of Edward's men fled, and he was captured at Olney and taken to Warwick Castle. However, without a firm plan, of how to dispose of the King, it seemed that the Earl could not raise enough supporters to remove Edward from the throne. Without their King, the country descended into chaos and Warwick found himself unable to regain control. Unable to bring himself to commit cold-blooded murder on his King and onetime close ally at this time, he embarrassingly had to let Edward go. Edward returned to London at the end of 1469. Edward 'in peace just and merciful' forgave Clarence and Warwick and they returned temporarily to the fold.

But behind the scenes they were still plotting and causing trouble, and in March 1470 Warwick and Clarence chose to openly rebel again. A private feud between two Lincolnshire Lords began to spill over, and Edward riding with his men to control the situation, discovered that some of the troublemakers were openly aligned with Clarence and Warwick. By May of that year, the pair realised that their treachery would not be forgiven so easily this time, and they fled to France, where the men of Calais, remaining loyal to their King, this time refused to allow them to dock. During this sea journey, Clarence's wife, Isabel, gave birth to a son, in what must have been horrendous conditions below deck. Eventually making shore further down the coast, Warwick met with Margaret of Anjou and made a deal that he would help restore her husband to the throne, if she agreed to a marriage between her son Edward and his youngest daughter Anne Neville, making Anne the next potential Queen of England. Margaret agreed and Warwick began preparations to sail to England with an army.

The vain and arrogant Clarence at this point began to suspect that his importance in these schemes was waning, now that the Earl was fighting to put Henry back on the throne rather than himself and Isabel. He was also under pressure from his family to remain loyal, particularly from his two sisters and no doubt his mother. Whilst still appearing to support Warwick on the surface, the Duke was 'quietly reconciled to the King by the mediation of [their] sisters, the Duchesses of Burgundy and Exeter'. The former, from outside the kingdom, had been encouraging the King, and the latter, from within, the Duke, to make peace.[2]

Warwick, having made his pact with Margaret of Anjou, set sail back to England and headed for London, his mission to free Henry VI from the Tower of London. October 1470 found Edward trapped, surrounded by rebels in the north and Warwick's army marching up from the south. He was faced with no choice other than to flee abroad himself with his most loyal supporters, including his youngest brother, Richard, Duke of Gloucester and William Hastings, his trustworthy friend and Lord Chamberlain. Queen Elizabeth, on hearing the news and heavily pregnant, fled into the confines of sanctuary at Westminster Abbey, taking her mother and three young daughters with her. Warwick returned to London, and in a period known as the re-adaption of Henry VI, briefly restored the old King to the throne. For the next six months, the House of Lancaster was back in charge of the country.

Edward returned to England's shores six months later, determined to win back his throne and restore his family to power. Landing in the north of England, several cities weary of trouble refused to admit him. As he had only a few loyal supporters with him, Edward knew he was not yet a match for his enemies and so declared himself loyal to Henry VI, and claimed he was only back in England to reclaim the York title that was rightfully his after the death of his father and elder brother. He began a slow march down the country, collecting men in support along the way. Hastings, had ridden ahead to his homelands in the Midlands and by the time Edward had reached Leicester, Hastings had gathered an army of over three thousand 'stirred by his [Hastings] messages sent unto them, and by his servants, friends and lovers, such as were in the country'.[3]

At this point the Earl of Warwick was in Coventry and when Edward reached there, he refused to engage in battle, awaiting as he was for Clarence to come with reinforcements. Edward bypassed him and continued his march south, meeting up with Clarence in Banbury, where George fell on his knees and begged forgiveness from his brother. Edward hugged him and immediately forgave him. The pair and their armies returned to Coventry but Warwick, presumably at this point realising he had lost the support of Clarence, still refused to engage. Edward's men left him there and began to march on London to reclaim the capital.

It is worth a mention at this point that unlike Edward's wayward brother, Clarence, his younger brother, Richard, had remained one of Edward's most trustworthy supporters throughout of all the troubles, and would remain so throughout the rest of his life. By his side in exile and in battle, it is this that makes his future actions in 1483 (discussed throughout the rest of the book) all the more perplexing.

On Tuesday 9th April 1471, the City of London was aware that 'Edward late King of England was hastening towards the city with a powerful army'. At the same time, Warwick was writing and urging the City to remain steadfast in support of Henry VI. With the Aldermen of the City in confusion and unsure of what they were supposed to do, the mayor, John Stockton, retired to his bed due to the stress and could not be persuaded to leave it![4]

Archbishop George Neville who was in London at the time, made a last-ditch attempt to persuade the people of London to remain loyal to Henry, by parading him through the streets. But the difference between the two Kings was striking – the old and fainthearted Henry VI, looking shabby in his old gown was no match when compared to the youthful, strong and popular Edward, and when Edward finally reached London, the gates were opened to admit him.

After greeting his wife and family and new-born son, born during his months in exile, and sending Henry back into imprisonment in the Tower, Edward was back as King of England. The Battles of Barnet and Tewkesbury a few weeks later saw the deaths of Warwick and Edward of Lancaster, the son of Henry VI and Margaret of Anjou. Margaret was also captured and taken to London and shortly after his return to the Capital after Tewkesbury, Henry VI was found dead in his room in the tower, supposedly of natural causes although undoubtedly few believed this official version of the story. For Edward and his family to be safe, the Lancastrian threat had to be removed once and for all.

Edward's second period on the throne of England was hard fought for, but by removing the threat from his enemies, he secured himself and his family a much more peaceful and secure reign from that point forward, albeit peppered with a few family squabbles. The years 1471 onwards encompass the childhood years of the York princesses, and are therefore discussed in more detail throughout the rest of the book.

Chapter One

Elizabeth of York

1466 to 1503

Elizabeth, whose fortune and grace was after to be queen, wife unto King Henry the Seventh and mother unto the Eighth.

Thomas More

On 11th February 1466, just under nine months after her coronation, Elizabeth Woodville gave birth to her first child with Edward IV, a daughter whom they named Elizabeth. The infant princess was born in the Queen's apartments in the Palace of Westminster, relatively new rooms in the rambling old palace which Edward had begun building for his Queen sometime after their marriage in 1464. Not long after her birth, the young Princess was baptised in St Stephens Chapel, Westminster, by Archbishop George Neville, a brother of the Earl of Warwick. Although she was a girl, and not the much longed-for son and heir that every King desires, she was, according to Agnes Strickland, baptised 'with as much pomp as if she had been the heir apparent of England; indeed the attention Edward IV bestowed upon her was extraordinary'.[1] Ever the proud father, Edward rewarded his wife for delivering him a beautiful daughter with a gift of a jewelled ornament, purportedly worth over £60,000 in today's currency to mark the occasion.[2]

As the eldest daughter of York, Elizabeth differs slightly from her sisters in that there is a wealth of source material on her. Although her destiny was ultimately very different from what her family originally planned for her, she would nevertheless go on to become the first Tudor Queen and thanks to her status, her life has been documented much more than the rest of her female siblings. Detailed and fascinating biographies have been written about her by authors such as Alison Weir, Amy Licence and Arlene Okerlund, amongst others, and for an in-depth look into her life they are certainly worth a read. For her chapter in this book, I intend to give a brief account of her life, focusing on some of the more intriguing details of her story.

After her christening, the royal trio settled into family life, with Elizabeth gaining two further sisters in 1467 and 1469 – Mary and Cecily. The Queen was yet to produce the much-required son and heir but was proving herself fertile. However, although life may have been rosy on the domestic front, outside events were beginning to disturb the equilibrium and by Elizabeth's fourth birthday her father's throne was in serious trouble. The danger to their family and the Yorkist dynasty as a whole may not have been fully understood by the young Elizabeth but she almost certainly would have been aware that something was not quite right – perhaps as grown-ups whispered in corners and her parents themselves appearing worried or distracted.

By October 1470, just a few months before Elizabeth's fifth birthday, Edward found himself with no choice but to flee his enemies and leave the country. On hearing the news and comprehending the danger she and her family were in, Elizabeth Woodville grabbed her three young daughters and fled into the sanctuary of Westminster Abbey, a fact that was reported by John Paston to his mother, Margaret, in a letter dated October 12th 1470. 'To my right worshipful mother, Margaret Paston, be this delivered. The Queen that was, and the Duchess of Bedford, be in sanctuary at Westminster; the Bishop of Ely with other Bishops are in Saint Martins. When I hear more, I shall send you more. I prey God send you all your desires. Written at London on Saint Edwards Eve. Your son and humble servant.[3]

After the execution of her father and brother in 1469, which had been carried out on the orders of the Duke of Warwick and George, Duke of Clarence, the Queen understandably feared for her safety. As it was, upon restoring Henry VI to the throne,

Warwick issued a statement that sanctuary was not to be breached 'upon pain of death' and the new Government paid Lady Scrope to attend the Queen in sanctuary.[4] But eight months pregnant, tired and worried, the Queen had every reason to doubt their sincerity and this proclamation by Warwick probably did little to ease their fears. The distress felt by her mother may have been obvious to the young Princess Elizabeth. As much as her mother and grandmother, Jacquetta Duchess of Bedford, may have attempted to shelter her emotionally, the news that her father had gone away, coupled with their new living situation, however much they sugar-coated it, would have been unsettling for a small child. These events in her young life would almost certainly have taught her some early life lessons that would no doubt have shaped her views on the world as she grew up.

Within the sanctuary confines, the Queen, or rather the 'the Queen that was' and her daughters had nothing else to do except wait for news and pray for the safe return of their father. News would have reached them of the attainment of their father and uncle, Richard Duke of Gloucester, and even the birth of a new baby brother for Elizabeth in November that year, poignantly named Edward in honour of his absent father, would not have improved the bleakness of their situation.

Whether the King and Queen were able to communicate during the following six months is impossible to know but they would not see each other again until the following April, when Edward triumphantly returned to London and the women were finally able to leave the sanctuary confines. With her father back on the throne in 1471, Princess Elizabeth would have entered a more stable period of her life. She was in attendance at many state occasions, including the reburial of her grandfather, the Duke of York which took place in 1476, and the marriage of her younger brother, Richard; both events were also attended by her sisters Mary and Cecily and are detailed in the next chapter.

Having rid himself of the troubles that haunted the first years of his reign, the court of Edward IV was relatively peaceful after 1471. Edward was a popular King as Polydore Vergil, an Italian Scholar who settled in England in the early 1500s noted: 'his kindness (which was very innate in him) [meant] that he existed on more familiar terms with the common run of humanity than the honor of his majesty dictated'. Vergil was commissioned to write a history of England by Henry VII and in it he describes Edward as 'tall and lofty of stature, so that he towered above everybody else. He had an honest face, happy eyes, a steadfast heart, a great mind, and a memory that retained whatever he had absorbed. He was circumspect in his actions, ready amidst dangers, harsh and fearsome towards his enemies, liberal towards his friends and guests, and very fortunate in fighting his wars'.

Elizabeth Woodville never achieved the same popularity that her husband did, in fact her reputation is often much maligned by later historians who would describe her as haughty and her Woodville family as upstarts and social climbers. But those views of her should of course be looked at in context and there is no question that she proved a loving and faithful consort to Edward, and together the King and Queen adored their ever-expanding family.

But there remained in the background an undercurrent of discord, in the shape of George, Duke of Clarence. Taken back into the fold by his brother after his disloyalty in 1469/70, George had celebrated along with Richard and Edward after their victory at Tewkesbury and appeared to settle into family life for a while, electing to spend less time at court and more time with his wife, Isabel, and their young family. However, shortly after giving birth to her fourth child in October 1476, Isabel died and this sent Clarence, either through grief or some other disturbance of mind, off the rails again.

Immediately after Isabel's death, George cited witchcraft, blaming one of his wife's servants, Ankarette Twynyho for her death, and accusing her of poisoning his wife. Much to the horror of her family, Clarence had her arrested and summarily executed immediately after a trial, during which he heavily influenced the jurors to pronounce a guilty verdict. Her family complained to the King and Edward attempted to reel his unruly brother in.

Clarence then sought the hand of Mary, the only daughter of Charles, Duke of Burgundy, and the step-daughter of his sister, Margaret (who had married the Duke in 1468). Edward refused, and according to Vergil, it was due to the obstruction of his marriage plans that 'the ancient hatred between these brothers (nothing stronger) manifested itself'. George took this rebuttal with ill grace and left court, refusing to dine with the King claiming he feared he would also be poisoned – this empty accusation also being directed at the Queen.

The troublesome chain of events continued when three men were arrested, accused of plotting Edward's death. One of the accused was a close associate of Clarence, and all three were found guilty at trial. Two of the three were then executed for treason, the third narrowly escaping with his life. This should have been a warning to Clarence, but he didn't take it. Instead he elected to align himself with a preacher, who happened to be a notorious Lancastrian, and burst into Parliament to protest the innocence of the condemned men, at the same time taking the opportunity to bad-mouth the King and disrespect the Queen and her family. Edward could not let this continue and found himself with little choice but to arrest his troublesome brother.

During his trial on charges of treason, Edward elected to personally question his brother. With the two pitted against each other the Croyland Chronicle reported that 'no one spoke against the duke but the king, and no one answered but the duke'. Clarence was convicted and despite desperate pleas for clemency by their mother, Cecily, for Edward to spare his life, on 18th February 1478, George Duke of Clarence, was put to death in the most infamous of executions, reportedly choosing to be drowned in a barrel of Malmesbury wine.

What would the twelve-year-old Elizabeth have felt at the death of her uncle at the hands of her father? She and her siblings were no doubt spared the details, but she would have certainly been informed of what had happened and given a reason why. In later years the Woodvilles would be blamed for Clarence's demise. It would be surprising if the Queen hadn't despised Clarence after her father and brother were put to death at his hands, but the decision to execute his brother, like so many others that the Queen was blamed for over the years, was ultimately Edward's alone. Edward could not have made this decision lightly, although George had been a thorn in his side for much of his reign. Their younger brother, Richard, Duke of Gloucester, who had always been loyal to Edward, was said to have been equally divided at this significant turn of events.

An old legend tells of a prophecy that Edward had consulted around that time, which was something he was allegedly prone to do in times of doubt. The tale was first mentioned by John Rous in his *Historia Regum Angliae*, written between 1489 and 1491 and apparently foretold simply that G would follow E (which was understood to foretell that after Edward, G would reign).[5] It is unlikely that Edward had his brother put to death solely on a prophecy, but it is highly likely that he took it more seriously than perhaps we would today. Coupled with everything else that he had to consider whilst deciding George's fate, he may strongly have felt that to protect his young son Edward's inheritance, he needed to rid himself and his family from the threat of G.

Vergil also mentions this prophecy, asserting that a rumour had circulated at the time that Edward had become frightened by a soothsayer's prediction that after him would reign a man whose name began with the letter G. Ironically, the prophecy did come true, but the G turned out to be his younger brother, Gloucester! Vergil noting the irony wrote: 'Because devils are wont to play their pranks to inveigle the minds of folk who delight in such illusions, they said that this prediction was not untrue, since after Edward the Duke of Gloucester occupied the throne'.

Having witnessed treachery and trouble within her own close family, Elizabeth, on the cusp of adulthood, must have given thought to the seriousness of her position and that of her family, and what steps she may one day need to take to protect herself. 'Uneasy lies the head that wears the crown', a phrase introduced by Shakespeare in his play Henry IV, highlights the responsibility held by Kings to make the right decisions and none more so than here when Edward has to end the life of his own brother to ensure the safety of his family, his heir and the throne of England. The actions that her father took in 1477/78 may have played a part in how Elizabeth herself would react when it came to protecting her own family and throne in the years to come, particularly against its greatest threat – that of the possible re-emergence of her brother, purportedly back from the dead.

Elizabeth's expected throne at that time of her uncle's death was not the English throne however, but the French one. Her father had gone to France in August 1475 with the aim of repeating the success of past Kings and taking French lands back under English rule. Things did not quite go according to plan. Abandoned by his allies, Edward's campaign resulted in him striking a peace deal with King Louis XI known as the Treaty of Picquigny. As part of the treaty, an agreement was made that when they came of age, Elizabeth would marry Louis' son, the Dauphin Charles. From 1475 onwards Elizabeth became known as Madame la Dauphine with the arrangement made between the French and English Royal Houses that as soon as she reached the age of twelve, Elizabeth would be sent to France to live at the French royal court.

She reached that age in 1478, when Edward called on Louis to honour the deal. Her dowry was paid, and dresses were made for her in the French style so she could be appropriately dressed for the French court. But Louis stalled. By the time of her uncle's execution in early 1478, she would still have had no doubt that she would one day be Queen of France. But continuing unstable relations between France, Scotland, Burgundy, Spain and England, meant that alliances were constantly being made and broken. Unbeknownst to Edward, Louis had been in discussions with the King of Scotland, to forge an alliance by marrying the Dauphin Charles to James III's daughter Margaret. Nothing came of these discussions but then in 1482 the French King changed tact again and reached an agreement with Burgundy, known as the Treaty of Arras. In accordance with this treaty the Dauphin would marry Mary of Burgundy's daughter, the two-year-old Margaret. Mary of Burgundy, Clarence's one-time sought-after bride, had married Maximilian in 1477. Maximilian would become the Holy Roman Emperor in 1493.

It was not until January 1483 that Edward discovered this alliance and he was understandably furious. Elizabeth in turn was humiliated. Even though it was not a personal slight, the couple had never even met, it was still something she had been planning for, for the last eight years. She was not the first girl to have her marriage negotiations fall through, and she wouldn't be the last, but this had been a great match for Elizabeth bringing with is as it did a future queenship. Especially for a seventeen-year-old girl, the rejection would have been crushing.

Before Edward could take this any further, tragedy struck. In April 1483 the King fell ill and died. What followed should have been a simple transition of power to his twelve-year-old son, Prince Edward. As the Prince was still a minor, the King had added a codicil to his Will, naming his brother, Gloucester, as Lord Protector until his son came of age. Upon his death, the Queen and Edward's closest friend and advisor, William Hastings, wrote to Gloucester to break the news. Richard replied proffering his loyalty to Edward's son and heir and then began the long journey down from his residence in the north of England to the capital. Simultaneously Edward's young son, now Edward V, was being escorted to London by his older brother Richard Grey, and his uncle, Anthony Woodville, Earl Rivers, who had been with the young prince at Ludlow.

On his route south, Gloucester was joined by Harry Stafford, Duke of Buckingham, who was the husband of Katherine Woodville and therefore uncle to the new young King. Gloucester and Buckingham met up with the Ludlow party in Northampton on 29th April and shared a meal with Rivers and Richard Grey who had ridden to meet them, leaving the young prince behind at Stony Stratford. By all accounts the meal was convivial, with all four men enjoying each other's company. The next day, 30th April, they all began their journey to meet up with the new King at Stony Stratford, eighteen miles south of Northampton. But Rivers and Grey never reached their destination, along the route the two dukes pulled their horses up and informed the pair that they were under arrest. They then rode off to meet Edward to escort him to London, ordering Rivers and Grey be taken to one of Gloucester's northern castles as prisoners.[6]

Hearing this news, and once again fearing for the safety of her family, Elizabeth Woodville fled into sanctuary for the second time, accompanied by her daughters, her younger son Prince Richard, and her eldest son, Thomas Grey. Agnes Strickland in her *Lives of The Queens of England* paints a mournful image of the widowed Queen 'sat alone on the rushes all desolate and dismayed. Her long fair hair, so renowned for its beauty, escaped from its confinement and streaming over her person, swept the ground'. For Princess Elizabeth, this was the second time she had seen her seemingly strong mother in distress and had fled with her into the abbey confines. But this time she would have felt the burden of responsibility to support her mother more keenly than the first time, when she was just a young child. During their first spell in sanctuary the Queen had been accompanied by her mother and the two women would have been a mutual support for each other. But Jacquetta Woodville had died in 1472, and as the eldest daughter, this time Elizabeth would need to be strong for her mother and her younger siblings.

In early May Prince Edward arrived in London, escorted by Gloucester and Buckingham, where preparations had already begun for the young King's coronation. However, on their arrival, the coronation was immediately delayed. At the end of May Gloucester was appointed Lord Protector, and on 10th and 11th June he wrote to the City of York and to Lord Neville (his mother's family) asking them to bring troops 'to aid and assist us against the Queen, her bloody adherents and affinity; which have intended and daily doth intend to murder and utterly destroy us and our cousin the Duke of Buckingham and the old royal blood of the realm'.[7]

For the women in sanctuary, this time there was no hope of Edward coming back to save them; the Queen and her daughters were on their own. According to the Croyland Chronicle, plans were being made for the Princesses to escape from sanctuary and flee overseas: 'There was also a report that it had been recommended by those men who had taken refuge in the sanctuaries, that some of the King's daughters should leave Westminster, and go in disguise to the parts beyond the sea; in order that, if any fatal mishap should befall the said male children of the late King in the Tower, the kingdom might still, in consequence of the safety of his daughters, someday fall again into the hands of the rightful heirs.'

If this were true, Elizabeth and her sisters may have been embroiled in escape plots and plans which would have perhaps been both exhilarating and terrifying in equal measure! But once news of these plans reached Gloucester's ears, he immediately turned the tower into a fortress, hiring a man named John Nesfield to 'watch upon all the inlets and outlets of the monastery, so that not one of the persons there shut up could go forth, and no one could enter, without his permission'.[8]

With one Yorkist heir in the Tower, Gloucester now needed to obtain custody of the other Prince before he could proceed any further, the ten-year-old Richard of York. Unlike 1470 when Warwick issued a statement that sanctuary should not be broken upon pain of death, this time it was decided that sanctuary could be breached if necessary, with the Star Chamber deciding that as children could commit no crime in which sanctuary may be needed, sanctuary therefore did not apply to them. The Archbishop of York took this news to the women, warning them that the young Prince could be taken by force if they could not be persuaded to hand Richard over into his care. The official story was that Richard was required as a playmate and companion to his brother, Edward, whilst he awaited his coronation. Knowing they would attempt to take him by force if necessary, ultimately the Queen had little choice but to hand him over and Elizabeth and her sisters had to say farewell to their brother, not knowing if they would ever see him again.

On the outside, appearances were continuing to be made for the preparation of Edward's coronation but at a council meeting on 13th June, Gloucester made a bizarre claim that his arm had been withered by sorcery and he laid the blame for that at Elizabeth Woodville's door. That same day, William Hastings, who was Edward IV's closest friend, and had now pledged his loyalty to his son Edward, was also put to death, without any trial. From their place of sanctuary, the bad news kept on coming as the women learned of the deaths of the Queen's brother and son, Anthony Woodville and Richard Grey, in Pontefract. Then came the accusations that Edward IV's marriage to Elizabeth was invalid as he was already pre-contracted to an Eleanor Butler, and the even more salacious rumours that Edward was a bastard son, a result of his mother's affair, a hugely controversial claim considering Cecily Neville, mother to Edward and Richard, was still alive. Finally, on 6 July 1483 Richard, Duke of Gloucester, was crowned King Richard III at Westminster Abbey in a joint coronation with his wife, Anne Neville, just a stone's throw away from where the Queen and her daughters were confined. By then, rumours must have reached the sanctuary women of the 'disappearance' of the two Princes, who had been seen less and less until finally not at all and were presumed dead. For all of them, this was a heart-breaking conclusion.

It was likely at some point after the coronation and certainly when it was believed that the two Princes had been killed, that the Queen began discussing a plan that would affect Elizabeth directly. A visiting physician to the sanctuary rooms, a Dr Lewis, brought messages from Margaret Beaufort, mother to the last Lancastrian claimant to the throne, Henry Tudor, who had spent a large majority of his life in exile in France. The plan discussed between the two women, would see an alliance between the Houses of York and Lancaster, uniting them by the marriage of Henry with Princess Elizabeth. Messengers were sent to Henry in France and at dawn on Christmas day 1483 in Rennes cathedral, in the presence of five hundred supporters, Henry Tudor made a public promise to marry Elizabeth as soon as he was King. He then began to plan his invasion.

As with her betrothal with the Dauphin, Elizabeth did not know her intended spouse so could have had no personal feelings for him. We cannot know how much Elizabeth was involved in these plans and whether she had any say at all, but arguably the anger she would have felt at the treatment of her family and the disappearance of her younger brothers would have given her a determination to see this plan through and reclaim what rightfully belonged to her and her family. All she had to do now was wait for Henry to do his bit and defeat her uncle to claim the throne.

By March 1484 it became clear that Elizabeth and her daughters would have to leave their refuge at some point. Elizabeth Woodville's detractors often cannot understand her decision to release her daughters into the care of the man whom it was alleged killed her sons, but ultimately what choice did she really have? The women could not live in sanctuary forever and who knew how long it would be before Henry Tudor made it back to England, and even if he did, he may not be successful; there was a chance their plan may never come to fruition. Before she agreed to leave, the Queen did put in place as much protection as she could for her daughters, securing a written promise from the King that they would not be harmed. Richard agreed to these terms and committed to paper the following pledge:

I, Richard, by the Grace of God, King of England and of France, and Lord of Ireland, in the presence of you my Lords spiritual and temporal, and you Mayor and Aldermen of my City of London, promise and swear verbo regio upon these holy Evangels of God by me personally touched, that if the daughters of dame Elizabeth Gray late calling her self Quene of England, that is to wit Elizabeth, Cecill, Anne, Kateryn, and Briggitte, will come unto me out of the Sanctuary of Westminster and be guided, ruled, and demeaned after me, than I shall see that they shall be in surety of their lives, and also not suffer any manner hurt by any manner person or persons to them or any of them or their bodies and persons, to be done by way of ravishment or defouling contrary their wills, nor them or any of them imprison within the Tower of London or other prison ; but that I shall put them in honest places of good name and fame, and them honestly and courteously shall see to be found and entreated, and to have all things requisite and necessary for their exhibition and findings as my kinswomen, and that I shall marry such of them as now be marriageable to gentlemen born, and every of them give in marriage lands and tenements to the yearly value of two hundred marks for the term of their lives; and in likewise to the other daughters when they come to lawful age of marriage if they live. And such gentlemen as shall happen to marry with them, shall straitly charge, from time to time, lovingly to love and entreat them as their wives and my kinswomen, as they will avoid and eschew my pleasure.[9]

On their initial release the girls went to reside with their mother, who was effectively kept under house arrest, but they were certainly at court for the Christmas of 1484 where one of the most puzzling and intriguing stories concerning Elizabeth apparently took place. For it was around this time that rumours began to circulate that the King was enamoured with his niece. Even more bizarrely, there is a train of thought as to whether, in fact, the attraction was mutual.

One source of this story was the writer of the Croyland Chronicle who tells us that during the feast of Christmas, 'far too much attention was given to dancing and gaiety, and vain changes of apparal presented to Queen Anne and the lady Elizabeth, the eldest daughter of the late King, being of similar colour and shape; a thing that caused the people to murmur and the nobles and prelates greatly to wonder thereat'. According to the writer of the Chronicle, even more sinister rumours existed that the King was anticipating either divorce or an early death of the Queen, so he could contract a marriage with Elizabeth.

Earlier in 1484 the King and Queen had lost their only child and the pair had been heartbroken. From the time of his death, Anne's health had suffered and during the Christmas celebrations, she was still in mourning. During the festivities, the King received news from his spies abroad that Henry Tudor and other York supporters who had fled to France to join him after Richard's coronation, would surely invade England the following summer. The King was aware that Henry intended to marry Elizabeth if his invasion was successful, and some historians surmise that it was for this very reason that Richard may have considered marrying Elizabeth himself. But as he was already married, this was problematic.

Throughout early 1485, the health of the Queen continued to deteriorate and on 16th March, during an eclipse of the sun, Queen Anne died. Because of the earlier rumours concerning Richard's plans towards his niece, the Queen's death led some to suspect she had been poisoned. But were these just rumours or was there any truth in this? Vergil, certainly believed that an attraction did exist, but only one way: 'The King, thus lowysd from the bond of matrimony, began to cast an eye upon Elyzabeth his nece, and to desire hir in maryage; but because both the yowng lady hirself, and all others, did abhorre the wickednes so detestable, he determyned therefor to do everything by leisure'.[10]

To our modern sensitivities, a marriage between an uncle and his niece would be unspeakable. Even in the fifteenth century, when it was not considered out of the ordinary to marry someone you were distantly related to, the possibility of a marriage between the King and his niece was considered objectionable. It certainly would have required a special dispensation from the Pope, but this was not unusual – Richard had had to write for a dispensation when he married Anne Neville because of their close affinity. But it certainly was not beyond the realms of possibility if both parties had been in agreement.

But was it even considered or was it simply rumour? The majority of Richard's council felt the need to discuss it and were horrified at the idea, including his closest friends and advisors, Sir Richard Ratclyffe and William Catesby, although some suspected that they mostly feared Elizabeth taking the throne because she may then have chosen to avenge the murders of her uncle Anthony and elder brother Richard Grey. But the council made it clear to the King in no uncertain terms that the public would never accept such an act, even presenting to him more than twelve Doctors of Divinity, who asserted that the pope could grant no dispensation in the case of such a degree of consanguinity.

Whether it was fact or rumour, Richard was eventually forced to make a public statement in front of the mayor and citizens of London denying that he had ever considered taking Elizabeth as his wife. But with so much effort put into the discussion of the subject, does that perhaps signal that it did indeed cross Richard's mind? One possible scenario is that Richard had considered it as a political move to thwart Henry Tudor's plans to marry Elizabeth. After the way Elizabeth and her siblings had been treated by the King, it would seem to be a safe assumption that Vergil was correct to write that Elizabeth must have found the idea totally abhorrent. But then there is the infamous George Buck letter which tells a completely different story.

George Buck was a historian in the late sixteenth and seventeenth centuries who wrote 'The History of King Richard the Third'. The work was completed by 1619 but did not get published before his death. His draft manuscripts were then used by his nephew, also named George Buck, who published them in 1646 under his own name. The younger George Buck was not well considered in the literary world, taking credit for work that belonged to his uncle and facing accusations that he was careless in his transcription of his uncle's original text and that he had invented sources.

In 1979, the editor, Arthur Kincaid, finally published an authentic version of Buck's original history, having meticulously gone through all Buck's original notes and sources. Central to this story is a letter that George Buck (the elder) had allegedly seen in a household cabinet belonging to the Earl of Arundel. The letter has never been seen again, leading some to doubt it ever existed. But if authentic, this extraordinary letter, written in the hand of Elizabeth to the Duke of Norfolk (an ancestor of the Earl of Arundel) is an astounding piece of evidence in the story of Elizabeth and Richard III. In the letter, written in February 1485, Elizabeth seems to ask Norfolk to be a mediator in 'the cause of her marriage to the King', who was 'her only joy and maker in this world', that she was his 'in heart and thought' and that she 'feared the Queen would never die'.

Apart from the doubt surrounding its authenticity, this letter has caused much controversy, mainly because the contents have been passed down to us incomplete. Buck, the Younger, wrote his own interpretation of the letter from his uncle's notes and

Arthur Kincaid, using the original manuscript has since put together a very credible interpretation of how the full letter likely read.

For those who doubt either the existence of the letter, or the interpretation of the letter, arguments are robust against the idea that Elizabeth would have ever contemplated marriage with her uncle. The most contentious part of the letter of course is that she asks Norfolk to 'be a mediator in the cause of her marriage to the King'. This does appear incriminating, however on 22nd March 1485, shortly after Queen Anne died, Richard had sent a gentleman named Edward Brampton to Portugal, supposedly to negotiate two marriages – one for himself with Joana of Portugal, daughter of King Alfonso, and the other for Elizabeth to a nephew of Alphonso, the sixteen-year-old Manuel, Duke of Beja.[11] Those arguing that the letter is not referring to a marriage between Richard and Elizabeth quite rightly point out that if a simple comma is inserted after the word marriage, the meaning of the sentence is changed. Elizabeth asks Norfolk to be a mediator 'in the cause of her marriage, to the King' – in other words she is requesting Norfolk to mediate on her behalf to the King in the cause of her marriage – possibly to Alphonso, and not to the King himself.

The phrase 'she fears the Queen would never die' also does not paint Elizabeth in a good light, if we assume she is hoping for the Queen's death so she can then marry Richard. But then of course, this can also be interpreted differently – Elizabeth may have witnessed her aunt suffering a slow and even painful death and be simply wishing to end her aunt's misery? And was Richard her only 'joy and maker in this world' and was she his 'in heart and thought'? Certainly, he was her only hope at that current moment in time of securing her a good marriage and perhaps she had a fondness for him that she had harboured since childhood even? Medieval language was also much more descriptive and 'flowery' than modern language, so perhaps this is not as much of a declaration of love as it first appears to be.

The truth of course will never be known, and this letter has been much debated over the centuries. The Richard III society has some interesting articles by Alison Hanham and Arthur Kincaid debating the letter. But for all the evidence that can be given to disprove any feelings between uncle and niece, there is always the small and intriguing possibility that Elizabeth, a young girl of just eighteen, who had recently lost her father and her position in life, did come to see her uncle in a different light. He was only thirty-two years old at the time and if, as some suggest, he made her feel special and told her he wanted to marry her, she may even have fallen for him for a short while. Whatever the truth of the matter, we can only now ever surmise.

What we do know though is that Richard's public denial at the time simply fuelled rumours even more. And if there were plans for them to marry, it became virtually impossible once the rumours of poison began. Fast forward over seven decades later, when rumours were rife concerning the relationship between Elizabeth of York's granddaughter, Elizabeth I, and her alleged lover, Robert Dudley. Many of their contemporaries thought that if he were a single man, the Queen would take him as her husband. So when his wife, Amy Robsart, subsequently died in somewhat suspicious circumstances, apparently after a fall down a flight of stairs, fingers were immediately pointed in the direction of Robert and even the Queen herself. A marriage between them then became impossible – the Queen could not align herself with allegations of foul play and Richard III would have faced the same dilemma.

After the public denial, Elizabeth was sent to reside at Sheriff Hutton where it is likely she remained and certainly where she was on 7th August 1485 when Henry Tudor eventually landed back on England's shores, in Milford Haven. Richard was expecting him. The two armies met at Bosworth field and after a fierce battle, Richard who fought valiantly was defeated. The reign of the Plantagenets had ended and the Tudor era had begun. Richard's battered and bruised body, some of its injuries obtained after his death, was hastily buried in the choir at Greyfriars church, Leicester, where he would remain until 2012 where he was eventually discovered as part of the excavations that have since made him famous once more as 'the King in the car park'.

If Elizabeth was harbouring any feelings for her uncle, his death must have come as a huge shock to her. Even if she had never considered him in a romantic way, he was still her family and his death may have been bittersweet. But putting her personal emotions aside, she now had her duty to do; as planned so many months before by her mother and soon to be mother-in-law. She was now finally about to fulfil her destiny and become Queen – not of France as she had once thought but of England.

On his arrival into London, Henry immediately sent for Elizabeth and as one of his first acts he repealed Titulus Regius, the act that had been passed by King Richard declaring the York children illegitimate. The new King dated his reign to the day before Bosworth, making traitors of anyone who fought on Richard's side. This repealing of the act was a double-edged sword for Henry. He appeared to have no knowledge of the fate of the two York Princes and assuming this to be true, by legitimising Edward's children, if one of the Princes had survived and re-appeared, they would have a greater right to the throne than he himself did. But, to marry Elizabeth and unite the houses of York and Lancaster, legitimising her was something he had to do.

Elizabeth and Henry's wedding took place on 8th January 1486. Elizabeth was nineteen, almost twenty, to her twenty-nine-year old groom. Her wedding dress was a gown of silk damask and crimson satin with a kirtle of white cloth of gold damask and a mantle furred with ermine.[12] Her loose blonde hair was threaded with jewels. But despite his promises to make her

Queen, it would be nearly another two years before Elizabeth received her coronation.

Their first child, a son, whom they named Arthur, was born on 20th September 1486 at Winchester, less than nine months after their marriage which may indicate that there was an initial strong attraction between the couple before they were married. Of course, Arthur may also have just arrived a few weeks early. As the new heir to the Tudor dynasty, the infant Prince was sent to a separate household in Farnham, where he would be cared for by a wet nurse, and nursery staff.

Although the houses of York and Lancaster were now united, there still remained a handful of disaffected Yorkists who although no doubt supported Elizabeth of York, and in some cases had real affection for her, would still have removed the Lancastrian Henry Tudor from the throne if the opportunity arose. The first threat to the Tudors came in early 1487 in the shape of a pretender, called Lambert Simnel, who claimed to be the Earl of Warwick, the son of George Duke of Clarence. As a male of the Yorkist line, his claim to the throne was stronger. Some threw their support behind this pretender, but he proved no real threat as the real Warwick, aged just ten at the time, was locked up in the tower. Warwick was an unfortunate casualty of events, considered by many to be a peaceful if somewhat simple lad, he was no real threat to anyone but due to his ancestry, Henry had no choice but to house him in the Tower precisely to keep him out of reach of any who may use him to further the Yorkist cause. To counter the claims of Simnel, Henry paraded him through the streets of London and the plot was put to rest. In a slightly more worrying turn of events, Elizabeth's cousin, the Earl of Lincoln, son of her aunt, the Duchess of Suffolk, fled abroad. His claim to the throne was weaker as it was through his mother's side (she was sister to Edward, Clarence and Gloucester), but as a strong and healthy twenty-seven-year-old male, he was still a contender in the eyes of the Yorkist faction.

Around the same time as the Simnel plot, Elizabeth Woodville was deprived of all her possessions at Sheen. She was allocated a small pension, considerably less even than she received from Richard III, and she retired to the Abbey of Bermondsey. This must have been hard for Elizabeth, who would no doubt have had no say in Henry's decision concerning her mother. Some associated Elizabeth Woodville with the Simnel plot, which if true must have been hugely upsetting to Elizabeth – any removal of her husband from the throne would also remove her position. Maybe this is where Elizabeth's experience with the events involving her uncle Clarence would do her well. She now had her own position and prospects to protect, along with that of her infant son. Would she also be prepared to take on her close family to do that?

On 4th June that year, the Earl of Lincoln returned to England's shores with an army and the support of his aunt, the Duchess of Burgundy. Henry considered him a real threat and called for Elizabeth and Arthur to join him at Kenilworth. Once again, Elizabeth was faced with the prospect of close family members taking up arms, not against her personally, but against her husband who even at this stage she may well have had real affection for. Lincoln and Henry met on the battlefield at Stoke on 16th June 1486; Henry once again triumphed, and the Earl of Lincoln was killed.

With all-known Yorkist threats out of the way, Elizabeth's coronation finally took place in November 1487. Accompanied by her sisters, she finally became the rightful Queen of England and the first Tudor Queen. Once again, we can rely on Agnes Strickland, who in her description of Elizabeth at her coronation paints a picture of a beautiful young woman: 'She was not quite twenty-two; her figure was tall and handsome; her complexion fair and brilliant. She had, besides, soft blue eyes and delicate features, set off by a profusion of yellow hair. Her costume on this occasion was a gown of white silk, brocaded with gold, and a mantle of the same material, bordered with ermine and fastened across the breast with gold cords and tassels. A close-fitting cap, formed of rich gems in a golden network, encircled her head, and her hair fell loosely around her shoulders'.[13]

To secure the future of their fledgling dynasty, Henry and Elizabeth needed to provide their heir with a good marriage. Negotiations began in March 1488 for the betrothal of the two-year-old Prince Arthur to Catherine of Aragon, one of the daughters of Ferdinand of Aragon and Isabella of Castile. Elizabeth did not seem to be quite as fertile as her mother, with the King and Queen's second child, Margaret, not arriving until 30th November 1489 at Westminster. She was christened Margaret, almost certainly in honour of her paternal grandmother, Margaret Beaufort. But it was on St Peters Eve, 28th June 1491, that their third and most famous (some would say infamous) of their offspring was born at Greenwich palace. Christened Henry after his father, he of course would go on to become the great Henry VIII, although at the time of his birth he was of course the second male child and therefore not destined for greatness.

All was going well for the new King and Queen, they had three children in the royal nursery and all Yorkist threats were either dead or contained. But then two months after Henry's birth, in August 1491, a young man of considerable refinement sailed into the Irish town of Cork, and would become perhaps the greatest threat that the court of Henry and Elizabeth would face. For according to this sixteen-year-old youth, he was none other than Richard of York, the younger of the missing York Princes. His appearance obviously caused a certain amount of worry in the English court but to Elizabeth and her sisters, it must have stirred up a real flurry of emotions.

From Ireland, 'Richard' set sail for France where he gained the support of the French King and he eventually made his way to Margaret's court in Burgundy, where it was reported that she was initially suspicious of her visitor, but later became completely convinced of his identity and welcomed him with great joy. It would later be laid at Margaret's door that she was in fact the power behind this 'imposter', even perhaps having instigated the whole idea.

Over the next few years, the existence of this 'pretender' caused a shadow over the English court as news reached them of his whereabouts and how he appeared to be collecting supporters on his travels, much like the Pied Piper. During this time, Elizabeth gave birth to her second daughter in July 1492. During her confinement her mother died, on 8th June 1492, and Elizabeth was unable to attend her mother's funeral. She named her new-born daughter Elizabeth, in honour of her mother. Sadly, this first Elizabeth Tudor did not live beyond the age of three, dying in 1495.

As well as the death of their infant daughter, 1495 brought more bad news when Henry's uncle by marriage, Sir William Stanley, was found guilty of supporting the Pretender. He had allegedly been heard to say he would not fight against him if he was the son of Edward IV (a position which in all probability many noblemen may have taken, albeit not spoken out loud). Henry had no choice but to arrest him and execute him for treason. This must have been a hugely embarrassing situation for Margaret Beaufort's husband, Thomas Stanley. As tensions heightened, Henry revealed that his officials had been able to identify the pretender as Perkin Warbeck, the son of a peasant couple from Tournai (in modern day Belgium). But even with his supposed identity revealed, he was still a magnet for any disaffected Yorkists and so much as Richard III did before him, Henry began to arrange marriages for all of Elizabeth's unmarried sisters so they could not be used as pawns in any political games.

In July 1495 the pretender landed in Deal. The men of Kent remained loyal to their King and chased him away. He subsequently made his way to Scotland where he was received with honours by James IV who allowed him to live at the Scottish court, treated him as he would a son of Edward IV and arranged a marriage for him with Lady Katherine Gordon, the daughter of the Earl of Huntly. He was still at the Scottish court on 18th March 1496 when Elizabeth gave birth to her third daughter, Mary, at Sheen. But by September of that year it was time for the Pretender to take his chance, or for Richard Duke of York to return to his homeland to claim his throne, depending on your viewpoint. With the full support of the Scottish King James, they invaded England but did not get far across the border before having to make a hasty retreat. It would be another whole year before Perkin tried again. When he did, this time he chose to set sail from Scotland and make land in Cornwall. The men of Cornwall, more disillusioned with their King than the men of Deal due to the high taxes that Henry's Government had been levying on them, allowed him to land and march northwards through their lands. Collecting supporters along the way, he declared himself Richard IV at Bodmin.

The threat had now become very real and the King set off to meet him with an army. As the King drew near, many Cornishmen began to desert – a charge of treason was too serious a penalty to risk. With his supporters fading away, Perkin knew his cause to be lost and went into hiding in Beaulieu Abbey, where he was finally captured. He was taken to Taunton and it was here on 3rd October 1497 that the Tudor King and the alleged York King came face to face for the very first time. Official records tell us he admitted his deception at this meeting when he was put face to face with men he should know, including Thomas Grey, Marquis of Dorset, his 'step-brother', and failed to recognise them. Neither did they admit to recognising him. But them some might argue, what good would have come of it if they had admitted to knowing him and he them?

Both Warbeck and his wife Katherine were taken back to court. Lady Katherine Gordon was made one of Elizabeth's ladies and Perkin was allegedly kept close to Henry, not exactly a prisoner but also not at liberty. Interestingly, there is no record of either Elizabeth or any of her sisters meeting him. They may well have done so and immediately known him to be an imposter but if this was the case, it would have been the best argument possible to contradict his story, but nothing to that effect was made public. Of course, the opposite is also true, that none of his 'immediate family' came out in defence of his cause. For Elizabeth to recognise him as her true younger brother, she would have been effectively ending her reign and that of any of her children. Did she refuse to meet him, did they meet and know that neither of them could help the other – that their past would have to be buried or was he simply everything the Tudor regime said he was – a fraud? Whatever the truth, this must have been a hugely emotional time for Elizabeth, and perhaps once again she had to call upon the memory of her uncle Clarence and how far she herself needed to go to protect those she loved the most? Would she deny her brother to protect the future of her own children? Perkin, or Richard, whomever he really was, would finally meet his end in November 1498, after having made an attempt at an escape. Finding himself back in the Tower, he was alleged to have plotted with the young Earl of Warwick and they were both arrested and executed for treason in November. Evidence strongly indicates that this final act of rebellion was almost definitely a set-up, which the poor young Warwick also found himself caught up in. In one fell swoop, the threat from any male Yorkists was over.

The new year, 1499, bought slightly more joyous events into Elizabeth's life when on Thursday 21st February, she gave birth to her third son, Edmund, at Greenwich. The marriage plans for her eldest son were also well under way and the finalisation of the treaty with Spain occurred in July 1497 when it was agreed that Catherine of Aragon would come to England in 1499, when she was fourteen years old. A month later, in August, Arthur and Catherine's formal betrothal took place at Woodstock, which would be followed in May 1499 with a formal marriage ceremony at Tickenhall Palace near Beaulieu, where the Spanish diplomat, Puebla, stood as proxy for Catherine. Then in May 1500, Henry wrote to John Paston, announcing that Catherine would be on her way to England and that he would like Sir John to greet her on her arrival.[14]

To our trusty and welbeloved knight, Sir John Paston.
By the Kinge.
1500
MARCH 20
TRUSTY and welbeloved, we grete yow well, letting yow wete that our derest cousins, the Kinge and Queene of Spaine, have signified unto us by their sundry letters that the right excellent Princesse, the Lady Katherine, ther daughter, shal be transported from the parties of Spaine aforesaid to this our Realme, about the moneth of Maye next comeinge, for the solempnization of matrimony betweene our deerest sonne the Prince and the said Princesse. Wherfore we, consideringe that it is right fittinge and necessarye, as well for the honor of us as for the lawde and praise of our said Realme, to have the said Princesse honourably received at her arriveall, have appointed yow to be one amonge others to yeve attendance for the receivinge of the said Princesse; willinge and desiringe yow to prepare yourselfe for that intent, and so to continue in redynesse upon an houres warninge, till that by our other letters we shall advertise yow of the day and time of her arrivall, and where ye shall yeve your said attendance; and not to fayle therin, as ye tender our pleasure, the honor of yourselfe, and of this our foresaid Realme.

Yeven under our signet at our manner of Richmount, the xx[ty] day of Marche.

Expected in England in early 1500, Catherine was somewhat delayed, not actually arriving in England until 2nd October 1501. She made her state entry into London on 12th November; Elizabeth and Henry were staying at nearby Barnards Castle and watched her state arrival from a house in Cornhill. The following afternoon, Elizabeth met her new daughter in law for the first time. Following a sumptuous wedding at St Pauls and twelve days of celebration, the newly married couple went to live at Ludlow in December 1501.

All was now seemingly well in the Tudor court. With her eldest son and heir now happily married and the future of the Tudor dynasty provided for, as well as most external threats removed, Elizabeth could now rest and enjoy the Christmas season, looking ahead to a peaceful and happy 1502. The new year bought with it a further marriage treaty, when on 24th January 1502 Elizabeth's eldest daughter, Margaret, was betrothed to the Scottish King, James IV.

But the wheel of fortune kept on turning and in February 1502 terrible news reached the court that Arthur was sick. Elizabeth of course would have been hugely upset by this news, and she reportedly paid two priests to make offerings at thirty-five important religious shrines. Then all she could do was wait. Finally, the most awful news reached them that on 2nd April. Arthur had succumbed to his illness and died. Both the King and Queen were stricken with grief.

An account of Prince Arthur's death and interment was recorded by Leland in his *De Rebus Britannicis Collectanea* and is a striking example of how close the King and Queen had become during their sixteen-year marriage. Leland tells us that when the King was delivered of the news of the death of his eldest son, he sent for the Queen, so they could share in each other's grief. Finding the King in 'naturall and painefull sorrowe', the Queen comforted him as best she could with wise words, reminding him that his Lady Mother 'had never no more children but him onely, and that God by his Grace had ever preserved him, and bought him that he was'. She also reminded him that 'God had left him yet a fayre Prince [and] Two fayre princesses' and that God was where he was and they were both young enough to have more children. On hearing her words, the King was duly comforted and the Queen departed to her chamber, where she broke down in such sorrow that her ladies called for the King, who in turn came and comforted her.[15]

What was to be the last year of Elizabeth's life is the one we get the best glimpse of her as her privy purse expenses have survived for this year. Since their marriage, the King and Queen had seemingly not spent much time apart, another indication that a real relationship had grown between them. But in 1502, Elizabeth decided to go off on a solo progress. Reasons behind this can only be guessed at, but the death of her son may almost certainly have been a factor. On top of this, her sister, Cecily, whom she was incredibly close to, was banished from the court around this time (details of which are told in Chapter Four) which may not have improved Elizabeth's sombre mood.

The Queen had always remained close to her blood family and was extremely loyal to them all. Many of her sisters had been with her at court at some point during her queenship, and in 1501 Elizabeth even took her half-brother Arthur Plantagenet into her service as her carver.[16] Arthur was a bastard child of her father's. An item in her accounts also show a payment made to a gentleman who supposedly sheltered her uncle Anthony in Pontefract, many years before. This payment to someone who was presumably a stranger to the Queen highlights Elizabeth's strong bond towards her kin:

Itm. To a man of Poynfreyt sayeng himself to lodge in his house Therl Ryvers in tyme of his deth in almous ... xij d. December. To a person in whose house Earl Anthony lodged at the time of his death in 1483.

A third factor that could have affected Elizabeth's frame of mind at the time occurred just before she set off on progress. According to Thomas More, a man named James Tyrell, who was being held in the tower on charges of treason, allegedly claimed during his interrogation that he had murdered the two York Princes. His confession has never been proven and he was unable to provide evidence of where the bodies lay, claiming they had been moved. How this supposed confession affected Elizabeth would depend on what she knew or believed was the fate of her brothers. But this, coupled with the death of her son and the loss of her sister's company, perhaps meant she felt the need to leave her life behind for a while, to take some time to heal and reflect.

Elizabeth began her progress from Windsor on 12th July, and headed for Woodstock, accompanied by her sister Katherine. From here she journeyed west into Wales, where on 19th August she arrived at Raglan Castle.[17] Raglan Castle had been the home of her aunt Mary Woodville, who had been married to William Herbert. It was now in the possession of her cousin, Lady Elizabeth Somerset (nee Herbert) and her husband, Charles Somerset.

After Raglan, Elizabeth continued onto Chepstow, also owned by the Herbert and Somerset families, before returning slowly back towards London. By 6th October, she had reached Minster Lovell, in Oxfordshire, once home to another of her aunt's, Katherine Woodville, and her husband, Jasper Tudor. After Jasper's death, Minster Lovell came into the Crown's possession.

She was back in Richmond by 25th November ready to spend the Christmas season with her husband – maybe some time apart had been just what she needed. Also, by this time, she was heavily pregnant. By 26th January, she had retired to her apartments in the Tower, ready for her confinement.

In the days before epidurals and painkillers, women used

herbs and relics to help them through the pain of childbirth. Elizabeth favoured The Girdle of Our Lady, which belonged to Westminster Abbey and the accounts show this was bought to her in December: 'Itm. To a monke that brought our Lady gyrdelle to the Quene in rewarde'. The girdle would have been kept on an altar until it was needed, which was installed in her private chamber and contained any other relics that were kept for use in her private devotions.[18] During labour, the girdle would have been placed over her stomach, in the hope that the pains of childbirth would be eased by the aid and blessings of the Virgin Mary. Traditionally women would take confinement several weeks before the birth but this time it seemed the baby came early, as just a week later, on 2nd February, Elizabeth was delivered of a daughter whom she named Katherine, perhaps in honour of her sister Katherine who had been her companion on her travels. A few days after the birth, Elizabeth fell ill and Henry sent into Kent for a Dr Aylsworth, a physician:[19]

Itm. To James Nattres for his costs going into Kent for Doctor Hallyswurth physician to come to the Queen by the King's commandment. First for his boat hire from the Tower to Gravesend and again 3s. 4d. Itm. To two watermen abiding at Gravesend unto such time the said James came again for their expenses 4d. Itm. For horse hire and two guides by night and day 2s. 4d. and for his own expenses 16d.

But even with the aid of a physician, time had run out for Elizabeth and she died on the anniversary of her birth, 11th February 1503, her thirty-seventh birthday. Her baby, Katherine, appeared in the accounts on 14th February but sadly followed her mother to the grave soon after.

Itm. To Robert Lanston for 4 yards of flanell by him bought for my Lady Kateryn the King's daughter ...

Although never seen as the most influential of Queens, Elizabeth's legacy was arguably the kindness she bestowed on everyone and the love that her subjects and her family felt for her. Without her, it is highly unlikely that Henry VII would have been accepted on the throne as easily as he was and although it began as a marriage born of necessity and convenience, it seems that the couple did truly come to love and respect each other. He was said to be heartbroken at her death and was never the same man after. Never an exuberant personality anyway, he became undoubtedly dourer and sterner after her death. Her son, who went on to become Henry VIII, reportedly said that the news of his mother's death was the worst news he ever received. It was Henry who continued the Tudor dynasty, taking the throne on the death of his father in 1509, and ensuring the fame and reputation of the dynasty for centuries to come. Although, arguably, the greatest Queen to be named Elizabeth was yet to come, in the shape of her granddaughter, Elizabeth I, it is Elizabeth Tudor's steely determination to do her duty, remain loyal to those she loved and to survive all that her young life threw at her, that shaped the beginnings of England's most renowned dynasty.

Chapter Two

Mary of York

1467-1482

This noble king....and their entire affection towards him had been to his noble children, having in themselves also as many gifts of nature... as their age could receive.
Thomas More

Eighteen months after the birth of their first child, the King and Queen were delivered of their second daughter, Mary, on 11th August 1467 at Windsor Castle. Her christening took place the next day, 12th August, with Cardinal Bourchier acting as one of her sponsors. The infant Mary was sent to join her elder sister, Elizabeth, in the nursery at Sheen under the care of their nurse, Margaret Lady Berners. On 9th October that year the Queen was granted £400 per year for their upkeep.

As royal children, the girls would have been brought up to learn manners and decorum, as well as the skills they would need to make good wives and mothers. Religion would have played a hugely important role in their upbringing and if their household followed that of their brother, Edward's, whose household routine has been passed down to us in a set of ordinances, they would have been bidden to rise early to attend matins. If you arrived late, you would spend the day on bread and water. After morning prayer, they would breakfast followed by morning lessons. Dinner would be taken at 10am, followed by an afternoon of recreation and/or further learning. Supper would be at 4pm and the girls would then have some leisure time, before retiring to bed by 8pm.[1]

After they had gone to bed, only their attendants were

permitted to enter their chambers. The outer gates to the palace would be closed at 9 or 10pm dependant on the season, and night watchmen would patrol several times throughout the night to ensure their safety.[2]

Mary's younger years would have mirrored that of her sister, Elizabeth, and as the two eldest, they may have had a close relationship. As the second child, Mary was very much considered the back-up to her sister, particularly when Elizabeth was engaged to the Dauphin in 1475. Their sister, Cecily, had already been affianced to the Prince of Scots two years previously and yet no plans were made for Mary, likely because if anything happened to Elizabeth, she would take her place.

In 1476, aged nine, Mary and Elizabeth attended an event of huge emotional importance to their father; the reburial of their grandfather, Richard, Duke of York and their uncle, Edmund, both of whom died before their birth.

Edward's father and brother had been killed after the battle of Wakefield in 1460 and in a gruesome celebration for the Lancastrians, their heads were displayed on the Micklegate Bar in York, mocking their defeat. Edward had never forgotten this and shortly after he became King in 1461, he had the heads removed and buried with their bodies in Pontefract. Fifteen years later, and finally firmly established on his throne, Edward was able to give them the burial he believed they so deserved.

The Duke of York's last journey had begun in Pontefract on Monday 22nd July and the cortege arrived at their destination of Fotheringhay seven days later, between the hours of 2pm and 3pm. The bodies had been accompanied all the way by Richard Duke of Gloucester, acting as chief mourner.[3]

Fotheringhay Castle was a favoured residence of the Duke of York and Richard of Gloucester had been born there. Finally able to bring his father and brother home, Edward greeted the hearses carrying their bodies with tears in his eyes at the entrance to the cemetery at Fotheringhay. At his side were his brothers and other male family members, including the Queen's brother, Anthony Woodville and son, Thomas Grey. Edward was wearing a dark blue habit and hood, the mourning colour for Kings.

The following day the funeral took place, which Elizabeth attended along with her sister Mary and her mother. Queen Elizabeth Woodville was also dressed in blue and it is likely the two Princesses were also. Three funeral masses were celebrated, and the Princesses followed their parents in offering Mass pennies at the altar rail. Afterwards followed a great feast, apparently attended by around 20,000 people, held in the castle and in pavilions erected in the grounds.[4]

As well as this solemn occasion, there were also joyful occasions to celebrate as well, which Mary would have been present at, a notable one being that of the marriage of her younger brother, the four year old Richard, to Anne Mowbray, who was just five at the time of their nuptials. The wedding took place on 15th January 1478 in St Stephens Chapel, Westminster. Mary sat with her two sisters, Elizabeth and Cecily. Also seated under the gold canopy with them was her father and mother, their brother Edward and the King's mother, to await the arrival of the bride. After the ceremony, their uncle Richard showered the waiting crowds with gold and silver coins before the wedding party went on to a banquet where the young Anne was announced as Duchess of York – her young husband had been created Duke of York when he was just nine months old. A few days later, a tournament was held at Westminster, followed by dancing in the King's chamber by the young Duchess and her sister-in-law's. Sadly, like her husband, Anne would never fully live the life of a Duchess of York, dying as she did a couple of weeks before her 9th birthday at Greenwich.[5]

Along with her sister, Cecily, Mary was honoured at a ceremony in 1480 when they were both made Ladies of the Garter. The Order of the Garter, created by Edward III and inspired by the Legends of King Arthur, originally consisted of twenty-four Knights and was reserved as the highest award for loyalty and military prowess. The Ladies of the Garter were generally members of the royal family or closely associated with the order by marriage. Her elder sister Elizabeth had been initiated into the order a couple of years before. The keeper of the Royal Wardrobe, Piers Courteys, had the care of the liveries of the brotherhood of St George and the Garter, for which he was paid a salary of £100 pa. In 1480 he organised for robes and hoods to be made for the three eldest York girls to attend the annual feast of St George at Windsor Castle. But although she was created a Lady of the Garter, it is reported that Mary was unable to attend the annual celebrations, perhaps due to sickness.[6] Was this the beginning of a more serious illness?

If she had been ill, it may have been thought at this time that she would make a full recovery as in 1481, marriage negotiations began for a marriage between Mary and Frederick I of Denmark, a younger son of King Christian I of Denmark and his wife Dorothea of Brandenburg. However these were reportedly not continued again due to the declining health of the Princess.[7]

Whatever ailed Mary, she sadly never recovered and to the sorrow of her whole family, she died at Greenwich in May 1482. There are two surviving accounts of her death and burial, with the date of her passing given as either the Monday or Thursday before Whit Sunday. Both agree on her burial dates though as 27th and 28th May 'in the towne' of Greenwich.

Her funeral is described for us in great detail in 'The Royal Funerals of the House of York at Windsor' by Anne F. Sutton and Livia Visser-Fuchs. On Monday 27th May, Mary's body was brought to the parish church of Greenwich. Four tapers were placed around the body and Dirige was sung by the Bishop of Norfolk, who also sang mass the following morning. The chief mourner was not identified, but it was very possibly her aunt, Jane Woodville, who is listed first among the ladies. Also present in the funeral party was her cousin, Joan, Lady Stanley, daughter of her aunt Jacquetta Woodville and another cousin, Dame Katherine Grey. This Katherine may have been of a similar age to Mary and perhaps was a childhood companion.

Dinner was served to the women at the palace and the mourners then set off to accompany Mary's body from the church to a chariot, which was adorned in black cloth. The chariot and procession left the church, heading south across the Thames at Deptford, before turning west towards St George's bar, at the boundary of Southwark. The cortege then turned south, heading towards Kingston-upon-Thames.

As was custom, the procession was met a mile outside Kingston by local dignitaries. All parishes were required to send out a party to honour the cortege and accompany the funeral procession through their parish, until the next location took over. The bells of each town would also be rung as the cortege passed through. It appears on this occasion, the parish of Wandsworth failed in their duty as they are specifically mentioned as not having sent out a party to accompany the procession. One wonders what sort of a reprimand they would have received for this!

The night of 29th May was spent in All Saints Church in Kingston-upon-Thames. The following morning, they continued their journey to Windsor, accompanied by twenty to thirty poor men carrying torches. As they neared Windsor, they were met by the Mayor and several other personages, who were accompanied by a group of young girls dressed in white linen and holding torches and white candles. On entering the town, they proceeded to the first gate of the castle, where they were greeted by the college of St George. At this point, all except the mourners departed and Mary's body was carried from the chariot to the hearse in the choir. In need of repast, the ladies took turns to stay with the body, while others ate in the Dean's House. After they had all eaten, Dirige was sung by the Bishop of Chichester, and Mary was then laid to rest next to her brother, George, who had died in 1479 aged just two years old.

The following day masses were said for her soul. Alms were distributed to the poor, as was customary – the prayers of the poor were considered hugely important for easing the passage of the soul through purgatory.

The King and Queen and none of Mary's immediate family attended her funeral but this was not unusual. Mary was the third child that they had lost, but her death would have perhaps been felt more keenly by her parents and siblings as she had lived into her teenage years and they would have known and loved her dearly. Her father had intended St George's chapel to become the family mausoleum since the early 1470s and he had loved Windsor Castle, lavishing plenty of money and attention on it. The chapel was the seat of his esteemed Order of the Garter and was dedicated to St George. Both of Mary's parents would join her here in their final resting places, her father unexpectedly less than a year later.

Mary led only a short life but was saved all the turmoil that followed after the death of her father. Her coffin was discovered and opened during excavations in 1810 when a vault was under construction for the family of George III. Her body was well-preserved, enveloped in numerous folds of strong cere-cloth, closely packed with cords. She was revealed to have long, pale blond hair, a family trait it appears, and blue eyes which were open but disintegrated immediately when exposed to the air. Observers could see that she had been beautiful, an attribute that has been showered upon all of the York Princesses. Thanks to the chapel's redevelopment, begun by her father and completed by her nephew, Henry VIII, in the sixteenth century, Mary now rests regally in the company of a multitude of other royals who have been laid to rest there over the centuries.

Chapter Three

Cecily of York

1469-1507

Cecily, not so fortunate as fair.
Thomas More

Cecily of York was born at Westminster on 20th March 1469 into what was becoming a seriously unsettled time for the Yorkist royal family. Her arrival would have been a welcome distraction from the rumblings of trouble that were seemingly ever present in spring of that year. As the third female child, the longed-for birth of a son and heir was not immediately forthcoming, but Elizabeth was proving herself strong and fertile and there would have been hope that a son would soon follow. Princess Cecily was likely named in honour of Edward's mother, Cecily Neville. To celebrate her christening, two barrels of hippocras and a pipe of Gascon wine were delivered into the King's cellar.[1]

But outside of this picture of domesticity, the disaffected Earl of Warwick was causing tension. Choosing to momentarily ignore the signs of trouble that were brewing, shortly after Cecily's birth, Edward and Elizabeth set out on planned progress to East Anglia, accompanied by his younger brother, Richard Duke of Gloucester, and Elizabeth's brothers, Anthony and John Woodville. The two eldest York girls, three-year-old Elizabeth and two-year-old Mary also travelled with the parents. Cecily at just a few months old was left behind in the royal nursery, presumably still in need of a wet nurse and considered too young to travel such a distance.[2]

But by the end of June, Edward realised he had little choice but to deal directly with the troubles in the north that were not abating. Gathering his men, he left Elizabeth to continue their progress and fulfil their commitments in Norwich. The city had gone to great expense to welcome the royal family. Elizabeth and her daughters arrived in Norwich through the Westwick Gate on 18th July, where they were greeted by a stage covered in red and green fabric, atop of which were angels and giants, with crests of glittering gold leaf. The royal entourage were treated to a pageant entitled 'Salutation of Mary and Elizabeth', presumably in honour of the Queen's daughters, before proceeding to the Friars Preachers, where another stage had been constructed and another performance was put on for them. This second performance was bought to an untimely finish when a deluge of rain sent the royal family scurrying to their lodgings.[3]

Just over a week later, on Wednesday 26th July, the Battle of Edgecote took place. News of the death of her brother and father, executed on Warwick's order after the battle, reached the shocked Queen a few days later. She and the two young princesses were escorted back to London by her brother Anthony, who had returned to Norwich at speed, avoiding Warwick's men, to ensure her safe journey back to the capital. In what must have been an arduous and emotional journey back to London, it must surely have crossed their minds that it was only by the grace of God that Anthony too had escaped a similar fate.

As the Queen and her two girls hurried back to London, they arrived back into the capital keeping such 'scant state' that the mayor and alderman voted to give her some wine ten days later.[4] Reunited with her youngest daughter, Cecily, Elizabeth would have no doubt hugged her tight, grieving for her family, worrying about Edward's whereabouts and with a fierce desire to keep her girls close against the danger that faced them. Elizabeth may also have been reunited with her mother at this point, both women comforting each other in their grief.

News would have quickly filtered down to the women in London that Warwick had succeeded in capturing Edward and alone in London, the next few months would have been a worrying time for the women at court. During this period of upheaval, a follower of Warwick produced some lead images that he claimed Jacquetta had made for the purposes of witchcraft and sorcery, supposedly using them to bring about the marriage of Edward to her daughter. Despite the shock of her recent bereavement, Jacquetta refused to be cowed by the accusations, and wrote to the mayor and the aldermen of London for their assistance, reminding them of a favour she had done them in 1461, when she had persuaded Margaret of Anjou to spare the city from Lancastrian destruction. Jacquetta had once been one of Margaret's ladies and they had reportedly become firm friends. The council agreed to come to her aid.

When Edward escaped captivity and returned to London in October 1469, he had to make a demonstration of following the law and in January 1470, Jacquetta went before the King's great council, where the witnesses back-pedalled, and she was acquitted. Jacquetta wisely insisted that her exoneration be recorded in the official records. Witchcraft was a dangerous accusation, levelled in the main against women, and once accused it was very difficult to prove your innocence.

Cecily, a mere child in the cradle, was completely unaware of all of this and the likelihood is she would also not have remembered much of the preceding years 1470-71, which included the period spent in sanctuary as a two-year-old toddler, with her mother and two older sisters.

From 1471 onwards, her father was safely back on the throne of England and her childhood became a little more stable. Cecily certainly played her role as a young princess of the court – she was present in 1476 at the reburial of her grandfather, the Duke of York, in Fotheringhay, and also attended the wedding of her younger brother, Richard to the five-year-old Anne Mowbray.

In 1473, negotiations were begun to arrange a marriage for Cecily. An agreement was reached between Edward IV and King

James III of Scotland that Cecily would wed James' young son, James IV when they both came of age. Seemingly, she was the first of Edward's daughters that he had started marriage discussions for; perhaps she was deemed the most suitable and the closest in age to her intended spouse (Cecily was four in 1473, the infant Prince of Scots just a year old) or perhaps Edward already had his sights on an even greater match for her two elder sisters.

In October 1474, a formal betrothal of the couple took place in Edinburgh, as part of a treaty between the two countries. Then on December 26th of that year, a ceremony took place in Edinburgh with a deputation standing in for Cecily and from then on, the young Princess was styled Princess of Scots.[5]

But soon, internal politics across the Scottish border would see Cecily used as a pawn in the marriage market. The current King of Scotland, James III, was an unpopular ruler, and taxes he enforced to raise money for the forthcoming nuptials of his son to an English princess were not well received. Animosity had existed between the two nations for a long while and an English alliance was not popular. But the betrothal held fast for several years until in 1481, James III began pressing Edward to send Cecily to Scotland. She was still only twelve-years old at this point and Edward, it seems, was hesitant to comply.

As well as being an unpopular ruler with the Scottish people, there was also discord between the Scottish King and his two brothers. This all came to a head in the late 1470s, when James had had them both arrested on charges of treason. John, Earl of Mar had since died, but Alexander Stewart, Duke of Albany managed to escape captivity and in 1482 he turned up in England at the English court. That same year, James III made an ill-advised border raid, followed by a swift apology soon after, but by then his disillusioned brother had managed to persuade Edward to switch allegiance to him. Edward agreed to support him and as part of the deal, he switched Cecily's betrothal from the young Scottish prince to the Duke of Albany. At twenty-eight years old, he was fifteen years older than his intended bride.

Edward sent a small force north, headed by the Duke of Albany and Richard Duke of Gloucester. When they arrived in Scotland, Albany made peace with James, as did Gloucester, and with supposedly normal business resumed, Cecily was once again promised to the future James IV. A short while later an attempt was made on the Scottish King's life and once again, the Duke of Albany sought Edward's support and protection. Cecily found herself once again promised to the Duke of Albany. Finally, in October 1482, Edward called off her betrothal once and for all.

How much Cecily would have been told of these negotiations we can't know but she must have been aware of some of the details. Although as a young girl, and especially a young princess, she knew her duty was to marry a man of her father's choosing, it must still have been a hugely unsettling and ever so slightly frustrating situation for her to find herself passed backwards and forwards between the warring Scots.

Just over six months after her engagement was ended, Cecily like the rest of her sisters, had her life thrown into even more turmoil on the death of her father. As one of the eldest children, she by very nature had spent more years with him than her younger siblings and no doubt loved him deeply. Fleeing into sanctuary with her mother, Cecily and Elizabeth as the two eldest girls (Mary had died in 1482), must also have felt some sort of responsibility to take care of their grieving mother and helpless younger siblings. Did the older girls huddle together in the corners of their enforced prison, sharing their grief and discussing their destinies and the fate of their brothers? It is likely that they were already close as sisters but this shared experience would have made them even closer still.

Nine months later, and what must have felt like an eternity to the teenage Elizabeth and Cecily, her mother had reached an understanding with Richard III and negotiated their exit from the Abbey confines. The York Princesses were released into the care of their uncle Richard, the man who had taken their brother's rightful place on the throne. The details of those fateful nine months are so confusing that we cannot possibly know their feelings towards their uncle and how much any of the protagonists knew or didn't know about the fate of the missing Princes. Either way, the five remaining princesses were now all that were left of Edward and Elizabeth's family, and that must have made them determined to stick together and support each other in whatever the future now held for them.

During their months in sanctuary, plans had been discussed by their mother for the union of Princess Elizabeth to Margaret Beaufort's son, Henry Tudor, heir to the house of Lancaster. Cecily, it seemed, formed part their plan B; if Elizabeth died before the union could take place then Henry had agreed to marry Cecily instead.

Richard III had become aware of this plot, which was presumably part of the reason he chose to keep the York girls close. The way for him to thwart this was to marry off the sisters so they were out of Henry's reach. This is what he chose to do, at least for Cecily, and in 1483 Richard found her a husband – the relatively low born Ralph Scrope of Upsall and Masham.[6] Ralph was possibly the second or even the third son or Baron Scrope of Masham, a gentry family in the north who had been neighbours of Richard when he lived at Middleham. On the death of the 5th Baron Scrope in 1476, his widow had made an indenture with Richard to place her eldest son, Thomas, who was an adolescent at the time, into his service. The family were known to Richard and were Yorkist supporters which made them an ideal family to marry Cecily into. But although they were a family of some standing, this marriage would have been hugely humiliating for Cecily as Ralph, who was one of the younger sons, was not likely to inherit the Barony and came with no money or property to his name. Even during the Scottish betrothal fiasco, Cecily always knew that she was intended to make a good match, so this marriage would have been a disappointment. The marriage took place in 1484 when Cecily was a mere fifteen and Ralph around twenty-three years of age. Nothing else is known of their time together, they presumably lived at court and depending on Ralph's character, Cecily may have spent as much time as possible out of his company as she could! Of course the opposite may also be true and the couple may have discovered an attraction existed between them.

A year later, in 1485, Henry Tudor finally landed back on home shores and after defeating Richard on the battlefield at Bosworth, Margaret Beaufort's and Elizabeth Woodville's plan finally came to fruition. Elizabeth and her daughters made their way to Coldharbour Place in London, where they resided under the care of Henry's mother until the wedding of Princess Elizabeth to Henry Tudor could be arranged. Much is made of Margaret Beaufort's austere and formidable nature and how she was the third person ruling England behind her son and his wife; some would even say she ruled the King on occasions! It is often inferred that her intimidating personality overshadowed her daughter in law, Elizabeth, although there is no direct evidence to give this credence. But over the next few years, Cecily and Margaret would form a close friendship, which perhaps began during this time spent at Coldharbour, during the first few months of the Tudor reign.

When her sister became Queen, Cecily was appointed as her chief lady in waiting. In those first few years she lived at the Tudor Court with her sister, and in 1486 her marriage to Ralph Scrope was dissolved by Henry VII. We can only assume that Cecily was happy with this arrangement, although again the alternative could also be true; she may have actually grown to like her husband, and the pair may have been torn apart by Henry's decision. Either way we shall never know. But back at court as an unmarried woman, Cecily had to rely on her sister the Queen for her upkeep. After the death of their father and uncle, Richard, Elizabeth and her sisters were co-heiresses to the Lands of Mortimer, Earls of March and Clare which belonged to the house of York. On his ascension to the throne, however, Henry VII incorporated them into crown lands, leaving all the York girls without dowries. Elizabeth had to support them from her privy purse and gave them £50 per year, supplemented by arbitrary gifts of cash whenever she could. When they married, she paid their husbands £120 for their maintenance.[7]

Cecily was to play an important role in court life, and although all the Queen's unmarried sisters waited on her, Cecily was primarily her chief attendant. On Sunday 24th September 1486 she attended the christening of Elizabeth's first child, the much beloved Prince and heir whom they christened Arthur. Cecily was given the honour of carrying the infant Prince into Winchester Cathedral. The heir to the Tudor throne was wrapped in a mantle of crimson and a cloth of gold furred with ermine, with a train. Cecily was attended by her eleven-year-old sister, Anne and supported by her stepbrother, Thomas Grey, Marquess of Dorset and her cousin, the Earl of Lincoln. Several hundred unlit torches, carried by esquires and yeoman, were borne before the prince. Behind then followed all the lords, ladies and gentlewomen. Cecily carried her precious charge through the cloisters into the church where her mother, Elizabeth Woodville was waiting for them. After the ceremony was over, she carried him out of church and returned him to King and Queen, who were awaiting the return of their son in Elizabeth's chamber. Elizabeth was wearing a rich gown and laying in her bed of state, her husband sitting next to her. Cecily placed him in Elizabeth's arms and according to tradition, Elizabeth was the first person to call him by his Christian name.

The next time we see Cecily at a state occasion is November 1487 when she supported her sister at her coronation. On Friday 23rd November 1487, the Queen, wearing her royal robes, left

Greenwich by water, escorted by the Lord Mayor, Sheriffs and alderman of London. Cecily and her sisters were with her. The next day, 24th November, her sisters dressed her for her state entry into London and there was a grand procession through the streets of the City. The Queen's train was carried by Cecily, and when the procession began, Cecily and her aunt, Katherine Woodville, the Duchess of Bedford rode together in the first carriage, directly behind the Queen. That night was spent at Westminster, and the following morning, the 25th November, Elizabeth, dressed in purple velvet, and her ladies proceeded to Westminster Abbey. Jasper Tudor, the Duke of Bedford and Katherine Woodville's new husband, walked directly in front of the Queen bareheaded in his rich robes of state, followed by the Queen and Cecily who once again in charge of carrying her train. Then came the Duchess of Bedford and other ladies, 'the Duchesses having on ther Heds Coronatts of Golde richely garnyshed with Perle and precious stones'.[8] The procession was hugely eventful it seems, with reports that amidst such huge crowds that had formed to try and cut a piece of the woollen floor covering that the Queen walked on (as was the custom), a number of people were killed: 'ther was so Hoge a people inordyantly presing to cut the Ray Cloth .... in the presence certeyne Persons were slayne, and the Order of the ladies folowing the Quene was broken and distrobled.[9] At the banquet that followed, Cecily shared the Queen's table with Katherine Woodville and the Archbishop of Canterbury.

After having her first marriage dissolved and seeing her sister now settled, Cecily must have wondered what the future had in store for her. She did not have to wait too long. Henry, perhaps with the advice of Margaret Beaufort, soon arranged a husband for her and in December 1487 she was married to a favoured uncle of Henry's, John Viscount Welles. The groom was thirty-seven at the time of their wedding, Cecily still only eighteen. The King and Queen were guests at the wedding.

John Welles was Margaret Beaufort's half-brother. His father, Lionel, 6th Baron Welles had married a Joan Waterton, and with her he had a son, Richard, who would become the 7th Baron Welles, and four daughters. After the death of his first wife, he took as his second wife Margaret Beauchamp, the mother of Margaret Beaufort. Together, they had a son – John.

John Welles had once been an ardent York supported and was in high favour with Edward IV; he was one of the men who watched over his body after his death. Presumably his loyalty passing to Edward's son, he became disillusioned with the actions of Richard III, and sailed to France to join Henry Tudor in Brittany during Richard's reign. Welles remained in exile with Henry and returned with him in 1485. Knighted by Henry Tudor near Milford Haven on 7th August 1485, he fought alongside him at Bosworth and was created Viscount Welles sometime before 8th February 1486.[10] As mentioned previously, Cecily had a close relationship with Lady Margaret whom she would often visit at her home at Collyweston, and it may well have been Margaret's suggestion for Cecily to marry her half-brother.

The Christmas of 1487 was 'kept full honourably' at Greenwich and the newly married couple spent it with the King and Queen, the Heralds crying that year 'Laigesse, de noble Princesse la soeur de la Reyne notre soveraigne dame, et Countesse de Wellys.[11] The King presided over feasts in the great Hall and the Queen dined with her mother and Lady Margaret and Cecily 'the noble princess, sister to the Queen, our sovereign lady'. It may have been the first time they sat and reflected over the Christmases of their childhood, and where they now found themselves, back in their rightful place at the royal court. The royal party stayed at Greenwich for a week after Christmas and on New Years' Day gifts were distributed to the members of the household of the King and Queen as was custom. This was followed by a banquet.[12]

Now that Cecily was a married woman, she was replaced

as Elizabeth's chief attendant by her sister, Anne, although she surely remained close to her elder sister and the court. Outside of court life, Cecily and John were admitted members of the Corpus Christi Guild at Boston, Lincolnshire, which they joined in 1487. John Welles was alderman of the guild for a year in 1489.[13]

The couple's main home together appears to have been Pasmer's Place in St Sithes Lane, London. The house was owned by the Skinners Livery Company, and so named after its owner John Pasmer, who was a skinner and merchant adventurer. The house was rented out to John and Cecily and would have been conveniently situated for trips to and from the court. According to archaeological excavations in London, during the construction of Bloomberg's European headquarters, the area attracted wealthy merchants and many of their houses, including Pasmer's Place, were large buildings, with internal courtyards.[14]

The couple had two children together, Elizabeth and Anne Welles although sadly neither of them made it to adulthood. The ages they died are not recorded but one of the girls at least died before 1499. Then to Cecily's great distress, on 9th February 1499, her husband also died of pleurisy at his London home. In his Will, he left all his property to Cecily for the term of her life. He also requested that he should be buried wherever she and the King and Queen saw fit. Henry, on hearing the sad news, issued instructions that he should be buried in the old lady chapel at Westminster.[15] To add to her utter grief, it is said that her remaining child died shortly after.[16] Cecily was inconsolable.

Heartbroken, she returned to the Queen's household where she would have been certain of being lovingly comforted by her sister. The sisters had always been close, they had been through a lot together in their lives, and had shared losses, including their sister Mary, who was closest to them in age, and whose death may have bought them even closer together. They also it seemed shared a love of reading, as evidenced by their joint signatures in at least two books that they appeared to own together. The

Testament de Amyra Sultan Nichemedy, Empereur des Turcs has the date 12th September 1481 inscribed on the title page and is signed 'Elysabeth the Kyngys Dowther Boke' and 'Cecyl the Kyngys Dowther'. Along with Elizabeth, Cecily also inscribed the *Estoire del Saint Graal,* an illuminated manuscript of French romances which included the legends of King Arthur. As well as signing themselves 'the king's daughter', the book was also signed by "E. Wydevyll" possibly their uncle Edward Woodville or their mother Elizabeth Woodville before her marriage.[17] It is enticing to imagine the two princesses as young women, together in their chamber, reading the French romances and imagining their futures as Ladies of a King Arthur-style court.

Back in the royal circles, Lady Welles once again undertook key roles in family occasions. On 14th November 1501, the King and Queen's eldest son was married to the Spanish Infanta, Catherine of Aragon in a lavish ceremony at St Paul's Cathedral. Cecily, now thirty-two years of age, bore the train of the sixteen-year-old Princess. She was also present at the tournaments that followed, and records show that she danced with her nephew. She remained close with Elizabeth and on 13th May 1502 she lent her sister, the Queen, 3l 13s 4d.[18]

Sometime in 1501/2, Cecily finally chose to take her destiny into her own hands, and she fell in love with a gentleman called Thomas Kyme of Lincolnshire or the Isle of Wight. They married in secret, and when the marriage was discovered, a furious Henry banished her from court and confiscated her Welles lands. Thankfully for Cecily her friendship with the Lady Margaret remained steadfast and she offered the couple shelter at Collyweston. Margaret also pleaded with her son on her behalf and by 1504 she had persuaded him to return Cecily's lands to her.

When, where and how she met Thomas Kyme is not known, but he was a gentleman well below her status as the Queen's sister, so it was certainly a love match. One tenuous connection is that the Corpus Christi Guild that Cecily and John had belonged to in Boston, also had a connection to the Kyme family. The Guild was founded by Gilbert Alilaunde in May 1355, and their first decision was to keep a book listing all members, not by rank or seniority but by the date they joined. Between 1427 and 1440 a Thomas Kyme of Friskney was appointed a member of the Guild, and he held the position of alderman in 1447 – he may have been a possible relation to the Thomas that Cecily married. Incidentally Margaret Beaufort also became a member of the guild in the 1490s.[19]

This may have been where Cecily met Thomas, although it is believed that she did have a close relationship with her husband, John, so she may not have become aware of him even if she had met him here. He is also not listed as a member of the guild so it would have only been through other family members that they could have met.

Another more likely connection is through the Willoughby family. John Kyme of Friskney married Joan Willoughby and they had two sons, Thomas and John. It is this Thomas that is believed to have married Cecily. Thomas' mother, Joan, had a brother called John Willoughby. He was knighted by Edward IV and married a lady called Anne Cheyne. Together they had four sons and two daughters. Their eldest son, Robert, born c.1452, became the first Lord Willoughby of Brook.

This made Thomas Kyme and Robert Willoughby first cousins. Robert was Knight of the Body to Henry VII, Kings Councillor and Lord Steward of the Household. Robert and William (his brother) also participated in Buckingham's revolt and sought refuge in Brittany with Henry Tudor, fighting with him at the Battle of Bosworth. It is therefore not beyond the realms of possibility that Robert, who was certainly heavily involved with Henry and the court, may have been visited on occasion by his dashing cousin, Thomas, and in doing so, caught the eye of the Queen's beautiful sister, Cecily.[20] To further support the connection, Robert Willoughby had a son, also called Robert, born about 1470. This Robert married, as his second wife, Dorothy Grey, who was the daughter of Cecily's stepbrother Thomas Grey and his second wife, Cecily, so there were clear ties between the two families.

Where Cecily and Thomas lived after they had left Collyweston is unconfirmed, although several sources have them living on the Isle of Wight. There is a Manor House at East Standen on the Isle of Wight that purportedly belonged to a Thomas Cooke of Rookley, who married a Joan Howles. Allegedly during the Cookes tenure of the manor, they had some notable tenants – one Cecily and Thomas Kyme.[21] There is also a tale that Cecily bore Thomas Kyme two children, although evidence to back this up is scarce to non-existent. A possible clue that she had at least one daughter with Thomas, can be found in the Will of Lady Katherine Gordon, who was married to the Pretender, Perkin Warbeck. In her Will, dated 12th October 1537, she left 'such of my apparel as shall be thought meet for her...' to her 'cousin' Margaret Keymes (an alternative spelling of Kyme). This entry in Lady Katherine's Will is fascinating on two counts, firstly because it may prove the existence of at least one child born to Cecily and Thomas, if this Margaret is indeed their daughter. But even more interestingly, it points to a connection and possible friendship between Lady Katherine Gordon and Cecily that would most likely have started in 1497 when Katherine was taken to court along with her husband and given a place as one of Elizabeth's ladies. Did they become friends over their shared belief that Perkin was in fact Richard of York? Or did Cecily just form a bond with the lady who had been fooled by an imposter?[22]

It is of course highly feasible that Cecily did produce further children, the couple were assuredly in love and Cecily was only in her early thirties, so still of child-bearing age, but no further details can be found about Margaret or any other child she may have born to Thomas. After her earlier losses, she would certainly have been well deserving of a second chance at motherhood.

Cecily did make one more return to the public scene, when her sister the Queen died in February 1503. She was not present at her sister's lying-in-state, this role was covered by her sister Katherine, the disgraced Cecily perhaps still not forgiven enough to be allowed this honour. She was however one of the mourners at the funeral, perhaps signifying that in their shared grief, Henry relented and allowed her to return to court to mourn her sister.

After this, Cecily disappears from the records completely. Hopefully after all the sadness she had experienced, she finally found happiness with Thomas and a more peaceful life in their few short years together, although it may have been tinged with a sadness at the separation from her beloved elder sister at the end of her life.

Cecily reportedly died on 24th August 1507 and records are divided concerning her final resting place. Quarr Abbey, a Cistercian monastery on the Isle of Wight is the place that it is most often mentioned as her place of burial, but evidence has since been found in the Beaufort accounts stating that she died at Old Hatfield House and was interred at 'The Friars'. Other sources state that she died at East Standen.[23] What is certain is that Margaret Beaufort, her lifelong friend, paid for her funeral.

There could, of course, be some truth in all those accounts. Old Hatfield House was owned by Cardinal Morton, Bishop of Ely, who was a close friend of Margaret Beaufort, so Cecily may well have been staying there in 1507, perhaps visiting Margaret and other family, when she died. The Beaufort accounts record her being buried at 'The Friary', which Alison Weir has pointed out may be the friary at Kings Langley where her ancestor, Edmund of Langley was buried.[24] But Quarr Abbey on the Isle of Wight, which was completely destroyed during the Reformation (a farmhouse is now on the site) was once a famous monastery, founded in the 12th century. Dedicated to St Mary Magdalen, the monastery housed Cistercians or White Friars.[25] Could this also have been known locally as the Friars? If so, perhaps Cecily had requested in her Will that she be buried on her beloved Isle of Wight, where hopefully she spent some happy years. Legend certainly seems to think so.

Chapter Four

Margaret of York

1472

This noble king....and their entire affection towards him had been to his noble children, having in themselves also as many gifts of nature... as their age could receive.
Thomas More

Princess Margaret of York was born at Windsor in April 1472, the fifth child and fourth daughter of the King and Queen. Sadly, the young princess did not survive past the end of the year, dying of natural causes at just eight months old.

The short period of time that she was on this earth, however, was a year marked with notable events in the life of the Yorkist royal family. After the troubles of the previous few years that had culminated in Edward having to flee the country and Elizabeth and her older daughters taking refuge in sanctuary, Margaret's birth would have been a joyous occasion, coming at the start of a new beginning for the York dynasty.

With an April birth date, Margaret's conception would have been sometime around July 1471. Her father had returned from the continent in March 1471 and had immediately made his way back to London to reclaim the capital, taking the hapless Henry VI back into custody before heading to the Westminster sanctuary for a joyful reunion with Elizabeth who during the past six months, had endured 'right great trouble, sorrow and heaviness, which she sustained with all manner of patience that belonged to any creature'.[1] After greeting his wife and hugging his three young daughters, he finally got to meet his new-born son for the very first time; Elizabeth had given birth to his namesake and heir in November 1470 within the abbey confines.

After a short stay in London of only a few days, Edward then headed with his army to Barnet, ten miles outside the city where, on Easter Sunday, the Yorkist and Lancastrian armies met on the battlefield. The result was a resounding victory for the Yorkists, and, in what must have been a bittersweet victory for the King, the Earl of Warwick, once Edward's most ardent supporter, was killed on the battlefield. But before he could finally rest safe on his throne, he had one more major battle to fight, against the Lancastrian Queen Margaret, who had landed back on the shores of England the very same day that the Battle of Barnet had been raging. With her son, Edward, by her side she was determined to defeat the Yorkist army and restore her husband, Henry VI, back to the throne of England. But fortune was against her; on hearing the news of her arrival, the King hurriedly raised another army and headed west from London, meeting up with the Lancastrian army at Tewkesbury where on 4th May 1471, Edward finally secured his throne, routing the Lancastrians, and capturing Margaret who was brought back to London defeated and broken at the death of her son, who had been killed in the fighting. She would remain in captivity for the next four years.

After all this turmoil, the King and Queen spent much of June and July at Westminster and Windsor, no doubt sharing stories of their time apart and re-establishing their household. On 11th June 1471, the infant Prince Edward was invested as Prince of Wales at a ceremony in Westminster abbey, followed by a great council meeting in early July where he was formerly recognised as the heir to the throne and allegiance was pledged to him by all the great and noble magnates of the land. The York star was on the rise again and news that Elizabeth was once again pregnant with Margaret would have bought further joy to the couple.

As a mother of four children already Elizabeth may have suspected she was with child again sometime around September, having missed a couple of her 'courses'; confirmation would have come around November, five months or so into her pregnancy when she felt the baby quickening for the first time.

The royal family ended 1471 at the Palace of Westminster, where the King and Queen took part in a second coronation on Christmas day and twelfth night in the abbey. Elizabeth, who was certainly aware of the new life growing inside her at this point, was experiencing tiredness and did not wear her crown.[2] The re-crowning ceremonies were a time of celebration for all they had survived over the past year, for the beginnings of Edward's second reign and for the new child they were expecting in the spring; the new year of 1472 would have begun with an optimism for the future.

The date of Margaret's entrance into the world is given as 10th April and numerous accounts state that she was born in Winchester. If this was the case, she was in Winchester without the King, who according to John Ashdown-Hill, who has put together a detailed itinerary of Edward's movements throughout his reign, has Edward at Windsor throughout March and April that year. That Elizabeth was also at Windsor and gave birth to Margaret there is backed up by a letter, written by Sir John Paston to his brother, also called John, at the end of April who after greeting his brother, and giving him news of several prominent persons whom have wedded or died, informed him that 'The Qween hadde chylde, a dowghter, but late at Wyndesor; ther off I trow ye hadde worde'.[3]

As Elizabeth began her confinement to await Margaret's arrival, the first event of 1472 worthy of a mention was already taking seed back in London, where her nineteen year old brother-in-law, Richard Duke of Gloucester, in scenes worthy of a Shakespeare tale, had rescued his intended bride from the clutches of her family and smuggled her off to a place of sanctuary, until the pair could wed.

Just twelve days after Margaret's birth in April, a papal dispensation was issued permitting the marriage of her uncle

Richard to Anne Neville, the youngest daughter of the recently deceased Earl of Warwick. The dispensation was required because of their shared ancestry: Richard's mother, Cecily Neville was sister to Anne's grandfather, Richard Duke of Salisbury. The dispensation arrived in England in June, although the marriage may almost certainly have taken place before then.

The Earl's widow, the Countess of Warwick, was still living in 1472, and had taken refuge in Beaulieu Abbey during the troubles of the previous year. By rights, the Warwick estates should have been hers, but as punishment for the actions of her husband she was refused her entitlement; a few years later parliament in an appalling move, would have her declared legally dead when they divided up the Warwick estates, even though she did not actually die until the early 1490s.

The Earl and Countess of Warwick had two daughters. The eldest, Isabel Neville was married to the middle York brother, George Duke of Clarence, who in 1472 held custody of the estates by right of his wife and was keen to keep them all for himself. Anne Neville was the youngest daughter, who had been married to the Lancastrian prince Edward in 1470, as part of her father's schemes to remove Edward from the throne and replace him with Edward of Lancaster, with his daughter Anne as Queen. After her husband's death at Tewkesbury, Anne Neville had been bought to London along with his mother, Margaret of Anjou, where she was placed into the care of her sister and brother-in-law.

With Clarence seemingly in possession of all the vast Warwick estates, a dispute arose between the two brothers, with Richard demanding his share of the lands, which were worth a considerable amount and represented significant wealth and power. With Richard wanting his share, and his brother George refusing to give them up, the brothers were set on a warring path, with King Edward having to act as mediator.

On arrival in London, Anne had been sent to live with the

Clarences at Coldharbour Place where, by all accounts, she was very unhappy. Legend has it that George became aware of his brother's intentions to marry Anne and tried to keep her out of his reach, one account telling of how on one occasion he sent her to the house of one of his retainers, disguising her as a kitchen maid so Richard was unable to locate her. This story may be fictional, but in truth George may have tried to limit their meetings as much as possible. The pair must have made contact at some point however and made plans, as on 16th February 1472, Richard enabled her escape from Coldharbour into the sanctuary at the London Collegiate church of St Martin Le Grand. A few short months later they were married.

Richard and Anne had known each other since childhood and much debate has been had over the motives behind their wedding. The romantics take the viewpoint that it was a love match, they had known each other for many years and the lovestruck couple plotted together to sneak Anne out of 'captivity' so they could be together. The cynical view is of course that by making Anne his wife, Richard had an even greater right to half of the Warwick lands, and this is often backed up by Richard's treatment of Anne in later life, as discussed in the chapter on Elizabeth. The truth probably lies somewhere in between both these versions, with the couple coming to the realisation that their marriage could be beneficial to them both. Despite an extreme version of events that exists that has Richard kidnapping Anne and forcing her hand in marriage, it appears Anne herself was no victim in this scenario and had been making attempts herself to regain her fortune and freedom, writing several letters to the Queen and her mother Jacquetta Woodville, as well as Cecily Neville, who all refused to assist her. Whatever the motives behind their actions, the marriage took place sometime between February and July 1472, based on the birthdate of their son, and the young couple went to live at Middleham, in the north of England, where they remained for the next ten years, with Richard supporting his brother in the management of the north. The matter of the Warwick estates would rumble on for another two years before parliament would pass an act dividing the lands equally between the two brothers.

The joy of Margaret's birth was followed a few short weeks later by sadness and grief, at the death of Jacquetta Woodville, who passed away on 30th May 1472. Jacquetta had been a rock to Elizabeth throughout her life, a constant support through the good times and the bad and Elizabeth would have felt her death keenly. Accounts of her funeral or burial place have not survived, with some historians surmising that she may have been buried at Grafton Regis. St Mary the Virgin church at Grafton Regis has a monument tomb to Elizabeth's great-grandfather, John Woodville, but as there is no mention of Jacquetta, it is unlikely she was buried there.

What is likely is that Jacquetta would have been afforded a funeral fit for a beloved mother of a Queen. Elizabeth had already lost her father some years previous; Richard Woodville, Earl Rivers, was executed in 1469 at Kenilworth by Warwick's men, and details of his final resting place are also scarce. Some accounts report that he was buried at All Saints Church, Pontefract. Elizabeth's brother, Anthony, who became the second Earl Rivers upon the death of his father, would many years later be executed and buried at Pontefract, so this may be where the confusion has arisen. It would make more sense for Richard Woodville to have been buried near Kenilworth.

In her Will, which also has not survived, Jacquetta may have requested to be buried alongside her husband, which many couples chose to do and still do today. She surely would not have wished to be laid to rest at his place of execution, so perhaps the couple now rest elsewhere.

In All Saints Church in Maidstone, there is a memorial stone set into the floor by the medieval screen. The tomb was originally one of three altar-tombs but now only rather unclear indentations at floor level can be seen. Two figures laying side by side can be seen but no lettering is visible. According to the church website, the two figures represent Richard Woodville and his wife Jacquetta – Richard on the left and Jacquetta on the right.[4] It is not beyond the realms of possibility that once Edward IV regained his throne in 1471, that he had the body of Earl Rivers bought here and reburied as a gesture to his wife; the Earl was born in Maidstone at Mote House so returning him to the place of his birth would not be unusual. Edward's own father, Richard Duke of York, was exhumed from his burial place in Pontefract and reinterred at Fotheringhay in 1476 so there is every chance he granted his wife the same favour, albeit on not such a grand scale as the ceremony that accompanied the Fotheringhay reburial.

Interestingly, the itinerary of Edward IV by John Ashdown-Hill places Edward in Kent on 15th June, just two weeks after Jacquetta's death, at the manor of Kennington. He then returns to Westminster before returning to Kennington again where he remains for much of July. Could this be that the royal family were in Kent for Jacquetta's funeral, remaining there for a few weeks to grieve and be close to her grave?

The above is of course all supposition, and to balance the argument, the tomb at Maidstone could also belong to Earl Rivers' father, who was also called Richard Woodville, and his mother Joan. They lived at Mote House and were very likely buried in the church, although they could of course still have been joined by their son and daughter-in-law later. Without further records being found, it is impossible to know where Richard and Jacquetta are buried, but if this is the final resting place of Richard Woodville, Earl Rivers, then it is highly possible that Jacquetta also lies here with him.

The third event worthy of a mention that occurred during the infant Margaret's short life took place in the autumn of that year and gives us a picture of the royal family at home, entertaining guests. During the months Edward had been in exile, he had been assisted by Louis de Bruges (Lodewijk van Gruuthuse), a Burgundian nobleman. Edward, in return invited him to England as an honoured guest and during his stay created him Earl of Winchester to thank him for his friendship.

Seigneur de Gruuthuse was accompanied amongst others by his son and by a manservant, Bluemantle Pursuivant, who left a detailed account of the visit. On arrival at Windsor Castle, the men were met by the Lord Chamberlain, William Hastings, who escorted him to meet the King and Queen. The Burgundian party were allocated three richly hung chambers to sleep in during their stay. That evening, the King accompanied Seigneur de Gruuthuse to Elizabeth's chamber, where the Queen and her ladies were playing games and dancing. An enjoyable evening was had by all, with the King dancing with his six-year-old daughter, Princess Elizabeth.

After mass the next morning, Edward gifted his visitor a gold cup, allegedly set with a piece of unicorn's horn, before presenting him to the Prince of Wales, who was not yet two years old. A young princess Margaret would have been completely oblivious to all the excitement of the visit but may have been proudly shown off to their visitor, along with the rest of the royal children.

During the rest of his stay, Seigneur de Gruuthuse was treated to a hunt, a walk in the palace gardens and a visit to the vineyard, before a banquet was again held in his honour in Elizabeth's chambers. The Gruuthuse's (father and son), sat with the royal couple at the main table, together with Elizabeth's younger sister, Katherine, the Duchess of Buckingham and her young husband, the Duchess of Exeter (the King's sister), and Princess Elizabeth. Courtiers and Gruuthuse's gentlemen sat at two other tables. Gruuthuse and his son were then taken to new and still more exquisitely furnished rooms, where they took a bath, Hastings bathing with them. The floor had been covered with warm towels, and the wooden tubs were placed under white canopies, a procession of servants needed to fill them with hot water from ewers. After bathing, the visitors were served with green ginger, comfits and spiced wine.[5]

The visit was a success and brought to an end an eventful year for the royal house of York, from the joy of a royal birth through to the sadness of the passing of the Queen's mother. The visit of the Burgundian gentlemen would have proved a welcome distraction from the family's grief over losing Jacquetta, but then as December came around a further tragedy struck. In a heart-breaking turn of events, the young Margaret of York, who had surely bought such joy to the family earlier on in the year, died on the 11th of December. This was an age where child death was not a rare occurrence, but still this was the first child that Elizabeth and Edward had lost and following so closely to Jacquetta's death, this would have been a real blow to the royal family. Details of her funeral, if they were ever recorded, no longer exist but baby Margaret was laid to rest in Westminster Abbey. Her tiny coffin was placed in the chapel of St Edward the Confessor, where her small altar tomb, now without inscription, can still be seen. Originally fitted into the steps of the shrine of Saint Edward the Confessor, it was moved at the time of the dissolution of the monasteries to the edge of the chapel. The step edging around the sides, however, can still be seen. The monumental brass which had been placed on the top of Margaret's tomb is long since missing, but the original wording was recorded historically:

Nobilitas et forma, decorque, tenella, juventus
In simul hic ista mortis funt condita cista,
Ut genus et nomen, sexum, tempus quoque mortis,
Noscas, cuncta tibi manifestat margo sepulchri[6]

There may also have been a verge inscription, also now gone:

Margaret, fifth daughter of the most illustrious Edward IV, King of England and France, and Elizabeth his Queen, his most serene Consort. She was born the 19th day of April, Ano. Dom. 1472, died the 11th of Dec, on whose soul God have mercy. Amen.[7] If this is a true depiction of the original inscription, then it would pinpoint Margaret's birth at 19th April, not 10th as believed.

Margaret's death bought the year to a sad end, but the deeply religious family would have grieved for her whilst taking some comfort knowing she was safely at rest in the arms of Elizabeth's mother. As she said a sad goodbye to her young daughter, Elizabeth may have been in the first few weeks of her next pregnancy, that of her second son, Richard, who would be born in August the following year, and would once again restore hope to the royal family as they ended 1472 and passed into the new year of 1473.

Chapter Five

Anne of York

1475-1511

Anne, that was after honourably married unto Thomas, then Lord Howard and after Earl of Surrey.
Thomas More

Princess Anne of York, the fifth daughter of King Edward and Queen Elizabeth, was born on 2nd November 1475 at Westminster. By the time of her birth the troubles of Edward's early reign were in the past and her father had firmly established himself on the throne; the future for the infant princess would have looked rosy. After her christening, she would have taken her place in the royal nursery along with her older siblings, placed into the care of a nurse called Agnes Butler. Agnes was awarded a pension in 1479, so likely remained with her young charge for the first few years of her life.[1]

In 1480, when Anne was nearly five years old, preparations began at the York court to receive a very special visitor in the form of her aunt, Margaret Duchess of Burgundy. With the exceptions of her elder sisters, Elizabeth and Mary, who both would have probably been too young to remember anyway, this was the first time that Anne and the rest of her siblings had met Margaret, although they may have heard tales of her from the rest of the family. Living as she now did in a far-off land, there was likely much excitement in the air for the York children, keen to meet their slightly exotic aunt for the first time.

Margaret was Edward's younger sister and had left England in 1468 at the age of twenty-two when a marriage had been arranged for her to Charles the Bold of Burgundy. Now aged thirty-three and a widow (her husband had died three years previously) she was one of the most influential women in Europe. Her trip had a special significance for Anne, although the young princess would not have appreciated it at the time, as part of the reason for her visit was to secure Anne as a bride for her step-grandson.

After the death of her husband, Margaret, who had formed a very close bond with her stepdaughter Mary, had been hugely instrumental in arranging Mary's marriage to Maximilian of Austria, future Holy Roman Emperor. Margaret and Mary had once looked to England for a suitable match, hoping to seal an unbreakable alliance with her brother's kingdom, but the only suitable candidate at the time had been George Duke of Clarence, and Edward could not and would not sanction the match. Mary had instead married Maximilian and it was their eldest son, Philip that Margaret wished to discuss as a suitable husband for Princess Anne.

So, it was in June 1480 that Margaret returned to her home shores for the first time since she had left twelve years ago. Edward Woodville, the Queen's brother, was dispatched to escort her home. Arriving in Calais in his ship named the 'Falcon', he collected Duchess Margaret and delivered her safely across the channel into the port of Gravesend. They then completed the journey into London by barge along the Thames.[2]

Edward was no doubt delighted to see his younger sister again, and he pulled out all the stops for her visit, beginning with an elaborate procession to celebrate her arrival. The royal barge that sailed her up the river was rowed by the master and twenty-four oarsmen, all dressed in smart new jackets of murrey and blue, embellished with roses. Once on dry land, she was transported to Greenwich by horses bedecked in harnesses of 'green velvet, garnished with aglets of silver gilt, bordered with spangels'.[3] Her homecoming was a real family reunion, as waiting to greet her was her brother the King and his Queen,

Elizabeth, Margaret's mother Cecily Neville, her brother Richard of Gloucester and her elder sister Elizabeth, Duchess of Suffolk. Princess Anne and the other royal children were also there to welcome her home. The only elephant in the room must have been the absence of their brother, George, Duke of Clarence.

Prior to her arrival Edward had given instructions that Greenwich Palace and Coldharbour House were to be prepared for Margaret's stay, two of her favourite childhood residences. Her first stop was to be Greenwich where she was escorted to her opulent chambers, hung with intricately woven tapestries and a feather bed with a valence of velvet. Pieces of woven wool tapestry covered the table containing images of 'roses, sunnes and crowns'.[4]

In her honour a banquet was held at Greenwich, hosted in their mother's name. Margaret was to remain in England until September 1480, during which time she and Edward had much to discuss, including her wish for England to support Burgundy against their troublesome neighbour France, and of course the terms of Anne's betrothal to Prince Philip of Austria.

Philip 'the Fair' or Philip 'the Handsome' as he was known was born in 1478 so was three years younger than Anne. Edward agreed to the match and signed the treaty on 5th August, vowing he would not promise Anne's hand to anyone else in the next three years. The marriage was to take place when Anne was twelve. The bride's dowry was set at 100,000 crowns and once she reached twelve years of age, Duke Maximilian would pay six thousand crowns a year for her support.[5]

But as with the planned marriages of her other sisters, none of this would actually come to fruition due to Edward's untimely death just three years later. Prince Philip would eventually go on to marry Juana of Spain, daughter of Ferdinand and Isabella and elder sister of Catherine of Aragon. Their marriage was fraught with drama and Philip was allegedly an arrogant and inconsiderate husband so Anne may have had a lucky escape!

Instead by the time she was twelve and should have been getting ready to travel to Austria, she found herself living at the court of her sister Elizabeth and her husband, King Henry VII.

Elizabeth obviously cared deeply for her sisters and became like a surrogate mother to her younger siblings. Our modern sensibilities might question why Elizabeth Woodville didn't keep the three younger York girls with her as opposed to leaving them at court with their sister, or in Bridget's case, placing her in the care of a priory. It was not unusual for royal children to spend substantial amounts of time away from their parents, raised as they were in the royal nursery or in their own separate household, so they would have been used to not seeing their parents on a daily basis. But more importantly, as a dowager Queen of an old administration, Elizabeth would have known that the prospects for her daughters would have been infinitely better at the new Tudor court. Now that their status had been diminished and they were no longer Princesses of the realm, they needed to be found good marriages to secure a good future and placing them in the care of the Tudor King and Queen would have been the best way to bring that about. Henry also had a distrust of Elizabeth Woodville, he was never completely sure of her loyalty, so he may have required the girls to remain at court where he could keep an eye on them and prevent them being used as pawns against him, in the same way Richard III had done in his reign.

Anne was very much involved in the life of the Tudor court, even from a tender age. In 1486, when she was eleven years old, she attended the lavish christening of her first nephew, Prince Arthur, playing a major role in the ceremony. The christening took place in the cathedral church of Winchester. Both the young Prince's chosen Christian name and the choice of location for his birth and christening, were designed to illustrate the power of the new Tudor regime. Winchester was the home of the legendary King Arthur, and by association it invoked a sense of awe and majesty that this new dynasty of Tudor Kings would bring to the country.

The church was decked out in all its finery, with the main body of the church awash with rich arras cloth that had been hung for the occasion. Arthur was escorted to the church in a procession involving all the great and good of the realm. Anne took her part in the procession, accompanied by Sir Richard Guildford on her right and Sir John Turbeville on her left, both bearing their staves of office. Pinned to her right breast and draped over her arm on 'a kerchief of fine ermines' was a rich chrisom to be placed on the anointed infants head. A chrisom was a square of white linen placed by the minister on the forehead of the child after the anointing oil. It was often allowed to remain there until the infant was a month old. Behind Anne in the procession came her elder sister, Lady Cecily, carrying baby Arthur.[6] The young Princess Anne must have felt very important with such a prestigious role to play!

After the christening festivities, the King, Queen and court moved to Greenwich where they celebrated the solemn feast of All Hallows. All Hallows was a precursor to our modern-day festival of Halloween and was followed on 1st November by All Saints Day. This was an important time in the medieval year when it was believed that during All Hallows Eve, the curtain between the physical and supernatural worlds was at its thinnest. The court then remained at Greenwich for the celebrations of Christmas and New Year.

Anne was also present at the first garter ceremony in Henry's reign which took place in April 1488. Queen Elizabeth and the King's mother, Lady Margaret Beaufort, rode together in procession through the grounds of Windsor castle in a chariot covered in cloth of gold. Anne rode after them, wearing a crimson velvet robe of the Order and accompanied by nineteen other ladies similarly dressed, on white palfreys with cloth of gold saddles. The Royal party attended mass at the castle followed by a great feast in St Georges Hall.[7] Anne herself was never made a Lady of the Garter; the last ladies to be introduced to the Order were her elder sisters Mary and Cecily in 1480. During this ceremony in 1488, Margaret Beaufort was invested as a Lady of the Garter but the tradition was then brought to an end for the next four hundred years. Future Kings and Queens did not have quite the same passion for this chivalric order as King Edward IV had had, and it was not until 1901 that Ladies would once again be invited to join, when King Edward VII invested his wife Queen Alexandra.

At the age of fourteen Anne once again took on the role of bearing the chrisom when the King and Queen's second child, Margaret was christened on 30th November 1489 at St Stephens Chapel, Westminster. Then two years later, at the age of sixteen, she had the heart-breaking task of acting as the chief mourner at the funeral of her mother, which took place in June 1492. The position would, in normal circumstances, have been filled by one of her elder sisters, Elizabeth and Cecily, but the Queen was in confinement awaiting the birth of her next child and Cecily's reason for absence is unknown. She may also have been expecting or perhaps in attendance on her sister, the Queen. On Tuesday 12th June, Anne and her younger sisters, Bridget and Katherine, travelled from Bermondsey to Windsor by water to pay their respects and to mourn their mother. Elizabeth was buried in St Georges Chapel, Windsor, alongside Edward, in a relatively low-key funeral for a woman who had been once been Queen of England.[8]

By the time of her mother's death, Anne held the position of Chief Lady of the Bedchamber at her sister's court, having taken on the role in 1487 from her sister Cecily, who left court after her marriage. But eventually the time came for Anne to be found a husband. The gentleman chosen for her was someone she may have already known as several accounts state that she had been betrothed to him once before, during the reign of her uncle

Richard. The gentleman in question was Lord Thomas Howard, son of the Earl of Surrey. He himself affirmed to King Henry that they had been betrothed since 1484. The young couple were married at Greenwich on 4th February 1495 when Anne was nineteen and Thomas was twenty-one. The King gave her away, making a gift of 6s 8d at their wedding which was listed in his privy purse expenses.[9]

The Howard clan were a rich and powerful family, who would arguably reach the peak of their influence during the Tudor era. Both Lord Thomas' grandfather, John Howard, and father, another Thomas, were trusted servants of Edward IV. After Edward IV's death, John and Thomas Howard had transferred their allegiance to Richard III; both were present at his coronation in 1483. Richard needed to swiftly establish himself on the throne and greatly needed the Howards support. As well as awarding them copious new manors to keep their loyalty, he created John Howard Duke of Norfolk and his son Thomas, Earl of Surrey. It may have been about this time that he also betrothed Thomas Junior (at that time aged ten), to the nine-year-old Anne of York.

Lord Thomas' father, Thomas Howard, Earl of Surrey was born at Stoke Nayland in Suffolk in 1443. In 1472 he married Elizabeth Tilney and together they were parents of eight sons and two daughters. Lord Thomas, Anne's new husband, was their eldest son.

Aged sixty and forty-two, both the Duke and the Earl fought on Richard's side at Bosworth. The Duke was killed during the battle and the Earl of Surrey wounded and taken prisoner. Attainders were bought against father and son during the first parliament of Henry's reign, which took place in November 1485, and they were stripped of all their properties and titles. Whilst his father was imprisoned, the young Thomas lived with his mother Elizabeth at her home of Ashwellthorpe, a manor in Norfolk that she had inherited from her father and that was not confiscated along with the other Howard properties. For some years she and her children lived in relative poverty.

The Earl spent three and a half years in the tower but his behaviour and determination to show that he would remain loyal to whomever was on the throne of England eventually earned him his release. Purportedly on one occasion he was given the chance to escape by one of the tower guards, but he refused to take it. Henry enamoured with his conduct agreed to meet him and upon doing so, consented to his release.[10] He left the Tower in January 1489 and the title of Earl of Surrey was restored to him. By rights upon the death of his father, he should have also inherited the Dukedom of Norfolk, but Henry was not prepared to be that generous. Some of his lands and properties were also returned and he began the slow process of earning back the rest.

At the time of Anne's marriage to Lord Thomas, Surrey was not yet in any position to bestow lands or riches on the newly married couple. The Queen could also not provide a dowry for Anne and as Henry would not bequeath the 10,000 marks promised to her by her family, the Queen and Surrey were left to reach an agreement between them to finalise the terms of the marriage. This they did and a marriage settlement was made by indenture dated 12th February 10 Hen VII, between the Queen and the Earl of Surrey. The Earl settled upon the marriage several manors which would come to the couple after the death of his mother, the dowager Duchess of Norfolk. The Queen for her part agreed to an annual payment of £120 towards the upkeep of her sister. She would also provide 20 shillings for meat and drink for every week of the year and cover the cost of the wages of two gentlewomen, a women child, a gentleman, a yeoman and three grooms. This was costed at £51, 11s and 8d for their wages, diet and clothing by the year. Also, from Elizabeth's privy purse would come the cost for the feeding and keeping of seven horses each year at £16, 9s, 4d.[11]

Elizabeth's privy purse expenses show a huge willingness

and generosity in support of Anne in her marriage. As part of the agreement, she also promised to cover the cost of Anne's clothing and items from her extant privy purse accounts show she did just this.[12] Her expenses from 2nd May 1502 detail a payment to William Botery for 'seven yards of green satin of Bruges for a kirtle for my Lady Anne'. At the same time Elizabeth ordered materials for her own gowns. The accounts also detail payments she made to Anne's husband:

March 1503. Itm. To my Lord Haward for the diettes of my Lady Anne for a yere ending at Mighelmas last passed.

It also appears than whenever she could she made gifts of money to her sisters, such as in February 1503 when she gave Anne a monetary gift:

Itm. to my Lady Anne for money geven unto hure by the quenes grace for hure purse for a yere ended at Mighelmas last past.

It was agreed that once the couple were married, as they had no income of their own, they would reside with Surrey and his wife in the various Howard properties. Two years after their marriage, Lord Thomas's mother, Elizabeth died and his father remarried her cousin, Agnes Tilney. Anne would likely have spent time living with both these women during her first years of marriage.

The young couple's main residence when in London was most probably Norfolk House in Old Paradise Street in Lambeth. The house was owned by the Earl of Surrey and was ideal for a courtier due to its location and proximity to the court. It was Surrey who built the Howard Chapel in St Mary's church Lambeth.

Lord Thomas's siblings would also become very much involved in court life in the years to come. His sister, Elizabeth, would marry Thomas Boleyn and become the mother of Anne, Mary and George Boleyn. His younger brother, Edmund, was the father of Katherine Howard, who would one day become the fifth wife of Henry VIII. It was here at Norfolk House that the young Katherine would spend her childhood, ostensibly in the charge of her step-grandmother, Agnes Howard. Katherine was not born until 1523 so although she was Anne's niece by marriage, the pair would never meet. But it was this property in Lambeth that became the scene of the crime after Katherine's arrest in 1541, when Agnes, by then the Dowager Duchess of Norfolk, purportedly had to rummage through the household coffers to remove any incriminating papers concerning her granddaughter and her alleged relationship with Francis Dereham.

The Lambeth house was quite a substantial property, When it was eventually passed out of the ownership of the Howards and was sold in the 1550s it was sold together with its outbuildings and lands and described in the bill of sale as a capital messuage 'wherin the ancestors of the said duke have accustomed to lye',' [that included by that time] 'two inns, formerly called the George and the Bell, the former being annexed to the mansion house on the west and the Bell, on the east; Bell Close, at the rear of the Bell, containing two acres, two perches; 23½ acres in "Cottmansfeld," an acre of pasture in St. George's Field, a close lying near the Bishop of Rochester's House (Carlisle House) containing four acres, three acres of meadow near Prince's Meadows, and eight acres of marsh called *the hopes*'.[13]

The land owned by the Norfolks, including the house itself, was so vast that seemingly the sale was divided into three parts, two-thirds of which were bought by one buyer and the last third, which included Norfolk House and the Bell and Bell Close by another.

Thomas and Anne would also have spent time at many of his father's other manors, including another London property in Tottenham. They also spent some time at Framlingham, which was an old Howard family property and was the preferred seat of the Earl of Surrey who died there in 1524, when he lay in state in the castle chapel for over four weeks before being transferred to the family mausoleum at Thetford priory. Framlingham's moment of glory came in 1533 when Mary Tudor raised her standard from the castle declaring her intention to take the throne, after the death of her brother, Edward VI, and during the very brief nine-day reign of Lady Jane Grey.

Two sets of accounts by the deer-keeper at Framlingham Park have survived dating between 1508-13 and 1515-19. In these accounts, nineteen entries between 1508 and early 1513 detail the activity of Lord Howard and Anne at the property. On occasions they were part of a hunting party, but the accounts show that Thomas and Anne also presented venison to local gentry with some frequency, taking on the roles in the absence of the Earl and Countess of Surrey. Anne presented gifts to a servant and local vicar and Thomas (no doubt with Anne by his side) entertained Lord Willoughby here and sent venison to various recipients, including the civic authorities of Bury, Norwich, Ipswich, Yarmouth and Bungay during or after his visits.[14]

Food was commonly given as a gift, and there are numerous accounts of Kings and Queens receiving gifts such as cakes, apples, oranges, and other fruit from their subjects. Food could be given as a small token of esteem or affection to a neighbour or a grand gesture from a gentry family and was almost always appreciated and useful to the recipient. Venison was a prestigious gift that indicated that the giver had a certain wealth and status in the area. The parker accounts are extensive and show that at Framlingham between one to two hundred deer were offered to dependents, local gentry and churchmen each year and that many were regular recipients.[15]

Anne and Thomas would also have spent periods of their married life together at Thomas' childhood home of Stoke Nayland. Thomas' grandfather, John, had built a substantial residence and household at Tendring Hall, Stoke Nayland, and this was his preferred residence during his lifetime. John Howard's income in the 1460s derived from his estates, from the sale of wool from over one thousand sheep. He was also a substantial ship owner, with at least ten vessels in his possession. The house itself no longer exists but some of the financial accounts relating to the household have survived from the periods 1462-71 and 1481-3. They paint a picture of an opulent Tendring Hall, furnished with tapestries, many embroidered with the Norfolk badge. In 1465 windows were inserted into the private quarters and beds and cushions were purchased for the family. On an expedition to Scotland in 1461 Duke John allegedly took with him many of his home comforts including carpets, curtains, sheets, towels, napkins, featherbeds, silver bowls and glass goblets. In the 1480s a chapel was built at the property, complete with an organ and hired choristers to sing. There was a harpist employed in his household in 1465 and seemingly at one point he also employed a troupe of minstrels.[16]

After being released from prison, it was to Tendring that Surrey returned and where he and his wife raised their children. In later years, he would relocate to Framlingham. That it was a favoured family property is illustrated by the fact that Lord Thomas returned to live there with his second wife in 1513, after Anne's death. He remained there until 1524, before moving to Kenninghall. A household book that has survived from the period illustrates in great detail the daily life of the family from this time and although it covers the life of Thomas and his second wife, it would not have been considerably different to Anne's time at Tendring.[17]

The accounts show that the Countess only ate fish on Wednesdays and on Friday the whole family followed suit. When Lord Howard and his wife were both at home, meals were served in the Lord's Chamber. When only the Countess was at home, dinner was provided in the Lady's chamber. Occasionally when entertaining, dinner was served in the great hall.

The number of people who usually dined at the Lord and Lady's table was between fifteen and twenty. Household meals were generally served in the hall where the gentlemen, yeomen and grooms were served. Mess was also held in the kitchen, the brewhouse, the bakehouse and the porters lodge. Dinner was at 10am; Supper at 5pm.

At Christmas the house was full, and sometimes sixty to seventy people upwards ate in the great hall. When the Earl of Surrey visited from Kenninghall or Framlingham, his servants lodged in the village and venison pasties were sent there from the main house.

The menu they ate shows a huge reliance on meat. For breakfast they would be served boiled capon, beef, mutton and chicken breasts. Dinner consisted of boiled capons, beef, mutton, a swan, a pig, a breast of veal and a custard for the first course. For the second course there would be six chickens, eight pigeons, five conies (hares), quails, pasties of venison, a tart, nuts and pears. Then again for supper the household would be served neck of mutton boiled, slices of beef, calves feet, shoulder and breast of mutton and a capon.[18]

After his father's death in 1524, Thomas gave Tendring to his brother, Edmund, and moved his household to Framlingham and then to Kenninghall, where he rebuilt the huge family mansion because Framlingham, like other castles had become outdated as a domestic residence.

During their marriage Anne and Thomas had four children but tragically none of them lived past a young age. The infants, who according to the Howard pedigree were named Muriel, Katherine, Henry and Thomas, were buried in the Howard Tomb at St Mary's Lambeth. This London church originally housed the fifteenth and sixteenth century tombs of many members of the Howard family. The building was deconsecrated in 1972 and due to be demolished but was rescued from that particular fate and the building now houses the 'Garden Museum'. The church contained now-lost memorial brasses to both Thomas Howard and his second wife Agnes (although they were not buried there) and is also the burial place of Anne Boleyn's mother, Elizabeth Boleyn (born Howard) who died in 1538.[19]

Out of all the four children born to Thomas and Anne, it seems that it was only their son, Thomas, who lived long enough to be baptised. As christenings usually took place shortly after the birth, we can perhaps surmise from that that the other three infants were either stillborn or survived only a few hours after birth. A missing brass, also from St Mary's was dedicated to their son and the inscription was believed to have read:

Here lies Lord Thomas, son of Thomas Lord Howard, and of his wife, daughter of Edward Fourth, King of England; which Thomas Lord Howard was son and heir of Thomas, Earl of Surrey, high treasurer of England. Died on 4th August 1508.[20]

The Howard property in Lambeth gave Thomas and Anne the opportunity to be near to the court. For Anne, this meant she could easily visit her sister and for Thomas, this gave him the chance to associate with the young Prince Henry. Although seventeen years older than Henry, Thomas became part of a group of men that would later form Henry's close circle and included Thomas Boleyn (husband of his sister, Elizabeth and the father of Anne Boleyn), Charles Brandon, the Marquis of Dorset (Anne's cousin, the son of her uncle Thomas Grey) and Henry Courtenay, who was married to her younger sister Katherine.

Anne mourned the death of her sister, the Queen, in 1503, and then in 1509 Henry Tudor also died and his throne passed to his surviving son, Henry. After the funeral obsequies were over, it was time for the new Tudor King to take his place and so it was on a midsummer's day in 1509, that an eighteen-year-old Henry and his new bride, Catherine of Aragon were crowned in a joint coronation in Westminster Abbey. Catherine had remained in England after the death of Henry's brother, Prince Arthur, and she married Henry shortly before the coronation. Anne and Thomas attended the festivities which went on for several days and brought with it a new optimism to the country. Henry Tudor had never really been secure on his throne, won as it was on the battlefield. He was always looking over his shoulder waiting for the next challenge from the old regime, the House of York. But his son Henry was confident of his destiny from the start and sure of his rightful claim to the throne. The old age of the great Plantagenet Kings had become a distant memory and the House of Tudor was here to stay.

In his chronicle of England written in the sixteenth century, Hall describes the preparations that were made for the coronation: 'If I should declare, what pain, labour, and diligence, the Taylers, Embrouderours, and Golde Smithes tooke, bothe to make and deuise garmentes, for Lordes, Ladies, Knightes, and Esquires, and also for deckyng, trappyng, and adornyng of Coursers, lenetes, and Palfreis it wer to long to rehersse, but for a suretie, more riche, nor more strauuge nor more curious workes, hath not been seen, then wer prepared against this coronacion'.

The celebrations commenced on 21st June when the King came from Greenwich Palace to the Tower. The next day, 22nd June, Henry invested twenty-four new Knights of the Bath. The day after that, which was a Saturday, Henry and Catherine left the tower and paraded through the city of London. The streets they passed through were hung with tapestries and arras cloth and the south side of Cheapside and some parts of Cornhill were hung with cloth of gold.[21]

All the great livery companies of London had turned out to greet them, dressed in their finery. Henry was attired in a robe of crimson velvet, furred with ermine. He wore a jacket of raised gold and a placard embroidered with diamonds, rubies, emeralds and great pearls amongst other rich stones. His knights of his body were dressed in crimson velvet and all his officers and household servants were wearing scarlet.

Behind the King's retinue came the Queen's, also richly dressed in cloth of gold or silver. The Queen was sat in a litter born by two white palfreys. She was wearing embroidered white satin with her hair loose and a coronet on her head set with rich stones. The following day, midsummer's day, the actual coronation was held, followed by a grand feast.

The coronation celebrations continued at the palace of Westminster with numerous tournaments and jousts over the following days. The jousts are described in great detail in Hall's Chronicle and Thomas and his friends took part in the celebrations: 'The enterprisers of these justes, was Thomas lorde Haward, heire apparaunt to the erle of Surrey, sir Edward Haward Admirall, his brother, the lorde Richarde, brother to the Marques Dorset, sir Edmod Haward, sir Thomas Kneuet, & Charles Brando esquire'. No doubt Anne was also there as part of the group of Ladies.

The new King appeared to hold his aunt in high esteem and on 23rd March 1510, he granted to Anne and her husband a messuage and garden in Stephenhithe (now Stepney). The following November he also awarded them several manors including the manor of Wingfield, with other manors granted to Anne for life with a reversionary clause in favour of her heirs.[22] The house at Stepney was most likely the property that had once belonged to John Howard and which had been confiscated from him after Bosworth. The house was situated quite far beyond the eastern walls of the city but was near to the parish of Ratcliffe which had thriving docks and warehouses. The Howard House stood in Bath Row. John Howard also owned the White Hart Inn at Ratcliffe where most of his men would lodge when the Duke was in residence.[23]

The date of Anne's death has not been recorded but it is believed she died sometime in 1512 when she was around thirty-seven years old. After her death, in early 1513, Thomas married Elizabeth Stafford, daughter of the Duke of Buckingham. With her he had two sons and two daughters. His eldest daughter Mary Howard married the King's bastard son, Henry Fitzroy, in 1533.

Both Thomas and his father maintained a close relationship with Henry VIII and after a victory against the Scots in the Battle of Flodden in 1513, Henry re-instated the Earl of Surrey with the Dukedom of Norfolk in early 1514 and Thomas took the Earl of Surrey title. Anne herself never became a Countess; she had only ever been Lady Howard. Upon the death of his father in May 1524, Thomas would go on to become the infamous Duke of Norfolk that we read about in our history books today, the scheming, cruel Duke who promoted two of his nieces, Anne Boleyn and Catherine Howard, to be Queens of England for purposes of family advancement and who callously sentenced his niece Anne Boleyn to death.

Anne of York was initially buried in the Cluniac Priory of Thetford after her death. The priory was founded in the early twelfth century by Roger Bigod and was the burial place of the earls and dukes of Norfolk for four hundred years. As well as Anne, her father-in-law, Sir Thomas Howard, was also buried at Thetford in 1524 and in 1536 when Thomas' son-in-law, Henry Fitzroy died, he too was buried there. But by the mid-1530s, Henry's chief minister, Thomas Cromwell, was beginning his scheme to close many of England's monasteries. In a bid to save his family mausoleum, the Duke proposed to convert the priory into a church of secular canons. In 1539 he petitioned the King to that effect and hoped that the fact that the King's own son lay buried in the priory would help his cause. He pointed out that along with the body of the Duke of Richmond, the King's natural son, the priory also contained the Duke's late wife, Lady Anne, aunt to his highness, the late Duke of Norfolk and other of his ancestors. Finally, he laid out his plans for setting up tombs for himself and the Duke of Richmond which would cost £400 and promised to make it 'a very honest parish church'.

At first the King listened but eventually Cromwell's arguments were more persuasive and the priory was listed to be closed. On 16th February 1540, Prior William and thirteen monks signed a deed of surrender.[24] Two months later the site and the whole possessions of the priory passed to the Duke of Norfolk for £1,000. Thomas arranged for the bodies of his family, and the Duke of Richmond, to be moved to a newly built chancel in the church at Framlingham. The priory of Thetford soon went into decay and the ruins today are under the care of English Heritage.

Thomas Howard in his position as Duke of Norfolk became part of the fabric of the Tudor court throughout Henry's reign, although he made many enemies along the way. Inter-court rivalry eventually peaked over who would become protector of Henry's young son and heir, Edward VI after the King's death. Edward's maternal uncles, Thomas and Edward Seymour clashed with Norfolk and his eldest son Henry, the Earl of Surrey. Thomas' son was not so politically astute as his father, and after some rash behaviour, charges of treason were brought against the pair. Surrey was executed and Thomas was thrown in the tower awaiting the same fate, escaping only because Henry VIII died the night prior to his planned execution. He languished in the tower for the next six years throughout the reign of Edward VI, until Mary Tudor, Henry's daughter by Catherine of Aragon, was proclaimed Queen at Framlingham itself. By this time, he had reached the grand old age of eighty, and after she released him, he retired to Kenninghall where he died within the year.

Upon his death, he was also buried at Framlingham, and his monument is the most outstanding one there. His tomb, surrounded by the figures of the twelve apostles, is immediately to the south of the high altar. It is known that there are two other male bodies interred in the same tomb, and they are believed to be those of his father and grandfather, that had been moved from Thetford. The female effigy on the tomb is almost certainly of Anne.

In 1841 the tombs were opened and six sets of remains were found which are generally believed to be those of John Howard, first Duke of Norfolk; Thomas Howard, second Duke of Norfolk; Anne of York, Lady Mary Howard, Duchess of Richmond, Henry Fitzroy, Duke of Richmond and the Duke of Norfolk himself. It has not yet, it seems, been proved conclusively which set of remains belong to whom. Norfolk's son by his second wife, Henry Howard, Earl of Surrey was also buried at Framlingham but his tomb is in a different part of the church.[25]

It seems hard to associate the man that Anne married to the man that he eventually became. The picture of the early years of Thomas and Anne as a young couple, sister and brother-in law to the Queen of England, starting out in their parental home and endeavouring to start a family paint a hugely different story to the hard-faced, severe and cruel reputation that Thomas Howard would earn for himself. Norfolk's relationship with his second wife, Elizabeth Stafford, was hugely volatile and the pair ended up hating each other. He kept a mistress, Elizabeth (Bess) Holland, for over fifteen years who had once worked in his wife's household and installed her at Kenninghall. Thomas and Elizabeth finally separated in 1534 and she retired to Redbourne in Hertfordshire, where she wrote countless letters to the King and Cromwell complaining of the wrongdoings of her husband, including that he was keeping her prisoner. She also complained that she was being physically mistreated by his servants and that the Duke had cut her head and 'he keeps that harlot Bess Holland and the residue of the harlots that bound me and pynnacled me and sat on my breast till I spat blood, and I reckon if I come home I shall be poisoned'.[26]

Anne, of course, only ever saw the glorious early years of Henry VIII's reign and never lived to witness Henry VIII's 'great matter', which culminated in his divorce from Catherine, his marriage to Anne Boleyn and the four other successive wives he took. Had she lived longer, and remained married to Thomas, would she have perhaps guided him to act differently, to navigate a less contentious and ambitious path through the Tudor court, or would she also have ended up shut away like his unhappy second wife? That of course, we will never know.

Chapter Six

Katherine of York

1479-1527

Katherine, which, long time tossed in either fortune, sometimes in wealth, oft in adversity.
Thomas More

In early March 1479, tragedy struck the royal House of York when two-year-old Prince George succumbed to 'an epidemic', as reported to his aunt in Burgundy and recorded by a Burgundian chronicler.[1] There was a serious outbreak of 'the great pestilence' in the spring of 1479 and George, it seems, succumbed to the disease. He was buried on 22nd March in St George's chapel, Westminster in an elaborate ceremony befitting a prince of the realm. At the time of his death, Queen Elizabeth Woodville was four months into her eleventh pregnancy so it must have been with some joy and renewal of hope in life that five months later, in August 1479, she gave birth to a healthy baby girl. Their daughter was born at Eltham palace, and they name her Katherine.

The princess Katherine took her place in the royal nursery along with the rest of her siblings under the care of a nurse called Joan Colson. Entries in the patent rolls for 1480 record an annuity of five pounds to Joan and her husband 'nurse to the King's daughter, Katherine' along with grants of land in Hitchin.[2]

Sometime shortly after her birth her father began negotiations with the Spanish King and Queen, Ferdinand and Isabella, for a marriage union between their son John, Prince of Asturias, and Katherine. John was the elder brother of Catherine of Aragon, and the couple's eldest son and their only son who would live to adulthood. Born in June 1478, he was a year older than his intended bride. But the negotiations came to nothing and John would eventually go on to marry Margaret of Austria, in a joint marriage deal that would see John's sister, Juana leave her Spanish homeland in late 1496 to marry Prince Philip, Margaret's brother. In turn in early 1497 Margaret left Austria for Spain where she would marry John. It was a good match and the couple appeared very much in love, although the marriage did not last long as sadly John died a mere eighteen months later.

Katherine was just four years old when her father died and only six when she entered the court of her sister, Elizabeth, where most of her childhood years would be spent. It was now the responsibility of her sister, the Queen, and King Henry to find Katherine and her siblings a suitable marriage. For Henry in particular it was important that they were matched with a husband who had proved their loyalty to him, so that the girls were not used as pawns in any political challenges for the throne. Their first choice of a husband for Katherine was James, Marquis of Ormonde and Earl of Ross, the second son of the Scottish King James III and in 1487 Henry opened negotiations with the Scottish King. However, these negotiations also fell through upon the death of James III in 1488.[3] But at the age of sixteen, a husband was found for her in the shape of the twenty-year-old William Courtenay, son of Edward Courtenay, Earl of Devon, and his wife Elizabeth. In October 1495 Katherine and William were married.

The Courtenay family had been Lancastrian supporters during the Wars of the Roses. The sixth Earl was taken prisoner after the Battle of Towton and executed in 1461. When Edward IV took the throne, the dead Earl was attainted, and all his lands became forfeit to the crown. During the reigns of Edward IV and Richard III, the attainted lands were distributed amongst other loyal peers or retained by the crown.[4] William's father, Edward, came from a junior branch of the family. He had also pledged his loyalty to the Lancastrians and had fled to Brittany with Henry Tudor, returning with him in 1485 to fight alongside him at Bosworth. That same year Henry had recreated him the 8th Earl of Devon and had restored the Courtenay lands to him, which included castles and estates at Plympton, Tiverton, Colyton and Okehampton, shops, cellars and tenements in the city of Exeter and numerous other estates such as Colyford and Kenn. Edward's loyalty to the Tudor King was therefore in no doubt and his son, William, had also been knighted at the coronation of Elizabeth of York.[5]

After their marriage, the young couple may have resided with William's parents for a while on their Devon estates. Together they had three children, Henry, Edward and Margaret who were all born in the few years after their marriage, Henry in around 1496, Edward c.1497 and Margaret sometime around 1499. For a while the couple remained in favour with the King and in 1497 William and his father assisted King Henry in Exeter when Perkin Warbeck besieged the city after declaring himself Richard IV. The King and his army raced towards Devon and in the meantime William and his father, along with another relation, Sir William Courtenay of Powderham, and various other men raced to Exeter to help the citizens. William was reported to have fought valiantly and in the skirmishes his father, the Earl, was hurt in the arm with an arrow.[6]

By 1500 William and Katherine had been summoned to court and took up residence in a property in Warwick Lane, Newgate, perfect for travelling back and forth to the royal palaces. William served at court and was granted an annuity in 1501 for his daily attendance on the King.[7] Katherine may have remained at home in Warwick Lane, bringing up her young children, but able to visit the Queen whenever she chose.

The property they lived in in Newgate was very possibly the house that once belonged to the Earls of Warwick, whom, according to the antiquarian John Stow in his 'Survey of London', the lane itself was named after. Previously called Eldenese Lane, it was the location of an ancient property which during the reign of Henry VI was reportedly occupied by Cecily, Duchess of Warwick and in the late 1450s, Richard Neville, Earl of Warwick, also stayed there 'backed by six hundred sturdy vassals, all in red jackets embroidered with ragged staves before and behind'. Stow's account also reports that 'there were oftentimes six oxen eaten at a breakfast; and every tavern was full of his meat, for he that had any acquaintance at that house might have there so much of sodden and roast meat as he could prick and carry upon a long dagger'.[8] With their own small family growing, and William holding a privileged position at court, all seemed to be going well for the young couple. But in 1502 things changed dramatically for the Courtenays when William was charged with treason.

Although the Yorkist threat to the Tudor throne had been dampened in 1499 with the execution of Perkin Warbeck, along with the young Earl of Warwick, Clarence's son, there were still occasional rumblings from other Yorkist males on the periphery who refused to completely accept Tudor rule. The main antagonist in 1502 was Edmund de la Pole, Earl of Suffolk, (son of Elizabeth Suffolk, Edward IV's sister) and younger brother of the Earl of Lincoln who had been defeated by Henry at the Battle of Stoke in 1487. Upon the death of his father in 1492, Edmund de la Pole should have inherited his father's title of Duke of Suffolk. Henry VII refused to grant him the Dukedom and only allowed him the title of Earl of Suffolk. Edmund had little choice but to accept this, but deep-down he carried a lot of resentment towards the King for denying him what he considered to be his rightful title. In 1498 Edmund had been indicted of murder in a fight and fled overseas, although he was afterwards pardoned for the offence. He did return to England for a short period, but then in 1501 he fled England's shores again, without royal leave, to his aunt Margaret's court in Burgundy. In the summer of that year in what was obviously designed to be a clear threat to Henry, he began calling himself the 'White Rose'. The King sent a gentleman called Robert Curson to investigate and it was he who discovered the plot against Henry and the throne. In response to this threat, Edmund was declared an outlaw and in February 1502 many other men were arrested suspected of their involvement in the conspiracy, including James Tyrrell, William de la Pole (Edmund's younger brother), Sir John Wyndham and William Courtenay.

Whether William was actually involved is doubtful, but he was part of a court circle that comprised Suffolk, his brother and James Tyrell and he was suspected of corresponding with Edmund and dining with him before he fled. But there was no direct evidence against Courtenay or William de la Pole and it is highly likely that they were arrested more for who they were than what they had done. With Katherine being a direct descendant of Edward IV, any suspicion against William put them in a dangerous position as they, as a couple, could be considered a direct threat to the Tudor throne. Out of those arrested, Tyrell and Wyndham were executed and William de la Pole would be kept imprisoned in the tower until his death, thirty-seven years later! As his punishment, William Courtenay was attainted for treason and put in the tower on charges of conspiracy. His estates were seized, and a clause stated that upon the death of his father they would revert to the crown. He would remain in prison for the rest of Henry's reign.[9]

The arrest of her husband must have been a terrifying set of circumstances for Katherine to find herself in, worried for her husband and even perhaps wondering if she herself would be suspected of involvement. Of course how much the couple knew and were or were not involved is impossible to know but for Katherine in particular, who it seems dearly loved her sister as much as her other siblings did, it would seem improbable that she would involve herself in a plot to remove her sister from the throne. She also now found herself in the situation, as many other women often found themselves in, of having to agonise about how she would look after herself and her children without her husband to support her.

Queen Elizabeth, it seems, may have had prior knowledge of Courtenay's arrest as a month before, she took the Courtenay children under her charge, paying for them to be bought from Devon to Havering, Essex, where she placed them in a nursery under the care of Margaret, Lady Cotton, with nurses and rockers for Edward and Margaret who would have been mere infants at the time. The royal house at Havering was a pretty house with a park that had formed part of the jointure of the Queen consort since 1262 when it had been granted to Queen Eleanor by Henry III.[10] One cannot help but wonder whether she also tipped off her sister at this time or whether she had to find an excuse to protect her niece and nephews; either way there would have surely been a battle of conscience between her loyalty to her husband and King and her sister. But Elizabeth was not going to let her younger sister live in poverty and after William's arrest, she took Katherine into her own household where she could care for and support her. Elizabeth had already been paying a pension of £50 to Katherine but now she also awarded her monetary gifts whenever she could.[11] The Queen, it seems, was also sympathetic to William's plight as her accounts from this time show that she paid for warm clothing to be sent to William in the tower, including a night cap, shirts and a 'half of fox for a gowne of russet'. She also covered the costs of the gown to be made.[12]

During her time at court, it appears that Katherine helped to raise Prince Henry, who would have been around the age of twelve at the time and the pair may have been close. He certainly held her in great esteem later in life and it may have been around this time that their relationship developed.

In the summer/autumn of 1502 Katherine accompanied her sister on progress, with Elizabeth paying for Katherine's saddle to be covered out of her privy purse. But then tragedy struck in July, whilst they were staying at the Abbots House at Notley Abbey in Buckinghamshire, when Katherine received the sad news of the death of her little son, Edward. Elizabeth's privy purse accounts show that the news arrived via a servant of Dame Margaret Cotton who was paid for his costs in coming from Havering to Notley to ask the Queen where Lord Edward should be buried (the accounts call him Lord Edmund, which is evidently a scribe's error). The Queen wrote to the Abbot of Westminster and paid for all his funeral costs, as detailed in her accounts, as well as gifts for his nurse and rocker:

> *March 1503. Itm. to Thomas Eldreton for the costs and charges of the burying of the young Lord Edmund (sic) Courtenay, son to the Lady Katherine, sister to the Queen. And for money by him given at the commandment of the Queen at the departure of the nurse and rocker of the same Lord.*[13]

Elizabeth's kindness to her family is undisputed and her care of her sister's children at Havering is a prime example. Her surviving accounts from the year 1502/3 detail several payments to Dame Margaret Cotton for their clothing, hose and shoelaces, and to a Mistress Cheyne for items bought for their chamber such as candlesticks. She also paid for all their food and an item in June 1502 shows a payment 'delivered to Dame Margaret Cotton for the diets of Lord Henry and Edward Courtenay and my Lady Margaret, their sister, two women servants and a groom'. Two more payments for food costs are made on 15th November 1502, the first identical to the May one for the diets of all three children from the last day of May to 13th July, and then a second payment made for the period 13th July to 2nd November that sadly omits little Edward from the list.[14]

It is not known whether Katherine left the Queen to continue her progress while she attended her son's funeral, or perhaps she visited her other children at Havering to share in their joint grief, but if she did she and her two remaining children rejoined her sister and the court at Christmas that year as the Queen's accounts from December detail a payment to Lawrance Travice for carrying 'stuff belonging to Lord Henry Courtenay and his sister Margaret from Havering to London'. There is also another payment to John Staunton the Younger for money laid out by him for horsemeat and the expenses of 'certain personnes' that bought Lord Henry and Lady Margaret his sister from Essex to London, and for his costs – a journey that took two days.[15] Christmas for Katherine and little Henry and Margaret must have been a bittersweet time that year, happy to be in the company of her sister and the court but also perhaps diminished by the loss of little Edward and the absence of her husband and the children's father.

Katherine was to receive even more distressing news in February 1503 when Queen Elizabeth died shortly after childbirth. This would have been a devastating blow to Katherine; as well as mourning the death of her sister whom she loved dearly, she must once again have felt hugely anxious and insecure about her own future and that of her children, now that her sister was no longer there to offer her protection and security.

At the funeral of her sister, which took place on 24th February 1503, Katherine acted as the chief mourner. The honour of that role should have gone to her elder sister, Cecily, but she had recently been banished from court and having spent much time in the last few months in the company of her sister, it was perhaps felt that Katherine was deserved of the role. On Sunday 12th February, the day after her death, Elizabeth's coffin was carried to the Church of St Peter ad Vincula within the tower, where she remained for the next eleven days. The coffin was carried under a canopy, held by four knights of the realm. Behind the coffin the Queen's household walked in procession. The stained-glass windows of the church were lined with black crepe and the walls hung with black silk damask; light was provided by five hundred tall candles. Katherine entered the chapel, accompanied by her brother-in-law, Sir Thomas Howard, and took her place at the head of her sister's body. She remained there during mass and for the next eleven days the coffin would be watched over at all times by six ladies in rotation. Other gentlewomen would give way to their betters, but Katherine herself was a constant presence kneeling at the head alone. As the Queen's death had been unexpected, the ladies wore the simplest clothing that they had, with kerchiefs on their heads until their mourning clothes were made.[16]

On the day of the funeral, the Queen's procession from the tower to Westminster followed the same route that she took for her coronation. Katherine was joined by her three sisters, Anne, Bridget and Cecily, all wearing mourning gowns with sweeping trains. Together they followed the chariot bearing the body of their sister and their Queen. After the service in Westminster Abbey, their nephew, the Marquis of Dorset, escorted Katherine, her sisters and all the lords and ladies to the Queen's great chamber in the palace of Westminster where Katherine presided over a supper of fish.[17]

Once the funeral was over, Katherine was sent to live with her father-in-law in Devon, presumably accompanied by her two children. Out of the sphere of the court, she falls out of the records for a while, living a fairly quiet life and raising her children. But then in 1509, the wheel of fortune turned once more, and Katherine's situation changed again when both her father-in-law and Henry VII died.

Upon the death of the Earl of Devon, his estates became forfeit to the crown as per William's attainder. The Earl had made provision in his Will for his grandchildren, ensuring that they received money from the Boconnoc estates, which were not part of the attained lands. They would both receive a share of one hundred marks a year; Henry until he was twenty-one and Margaret until she married.[18] The Earl's death could have potentially placed Katherine into a very tricky position, but the death of the King the same year was a stroke of luck for Katherine as unlike his father, the new King Henry VIII was willing and eager to protect his aunt in any way he could.

Upon his father's death, Henry VIII released William Courtenay from prison and at the same time reversed the attainder, granting him the Earldom which passed to him on the death of Edward Courtenay, and returning his lands to him. William, who most likely had known Henry since childhood, found great favour with Henry VIII and following his release he took part in the coronation jousts, celebrating the accession to the throne of the young Tudor King and his new bride, Catherine of Aragon. Back in the circle of the court, and back together again as husband and wife, the future was looking promising once more for William and Katherine.

On New Years' Day 1510 Queen Catherine gave birth to their first son, a prince whom they called Henry, after his father. Katherine attended the coronation as godmother to the child and more tournaments were held to celebrate the birth of the new Tudor heir and to honour the Queen. These took place on 11th and 12th February and the jousters assumed the role of olden day Knights. In the tournament, William took the part of Bon Valoyr, whilst the King was Coeur Loyall, Sir Thomas Knyvet was Bon Espoire and Sir Edward Nevil played the part of Valiant Desyre. Together they were called 'Les Chevaliers de la Forest Salvigne'.[19] Sadly a few weeks after these magnificent celebrations, and certainly before the end of February, the infant Prince died.

But life for Katherine never seemed to go smoothly and tragedy struck once more when in the summer of 1511, William died of pleurisy. The couple may once again have been residing in London close to the court as he died at Greenwich on Monday 9th June. His body lay in state until Thursday 12th before it was conveyed by river to his final resting place of the Blackfriars Church in London. Interred by especial order of the King, his funeral contained all the pomp and ceremony as would be expected at the funeral of an Earl. He was buried on the south side of the altar, but his grave is long-since lost as the church would later become a victim of the reformation.[20] But at the time of William's death, the Blackfriars had yet to stage it's most famous event; it was the location that Henry chose to hold the court that would hear his divorce proceedings against his Queen and the place where Catherine of Aragon famously made her impassioned speech to her husband, before turning around and walking out of the court, refusing to accept its ruling.

At the time of William's death, their son Henry was fifteen and became the new Earl of Devon. Katherine was just thirty-two. Henry's fondness for his aunt was once again demonstrated when in 1512 he granted Katherine all the Courtenay estates in Devon for the term of her life, and to be passed to her children upon her death. This act gave Katherine her much-needed security, although did she have to make a sacrifice to pay for it? For shortly after William's death, Katherine took the following vow of chastity:

In the name of the Father, the Son, and the Holy Ghost, I, Katherine Courtneye, Countess of Devonshire, widow, and not wedded, ne unto any man assured, promise and make a vow to God, and to our Lady, and to all the Company of Heaven, in the presence of you, worshipful Father in God, Richard, Bishop of London, for to be chaste of my body, and truly and devoutly shall keep me chaste, for this time forward, as long as my life lasteth, after the rule of St Paul. In nomine Patris et Filii et Spiritus Sancti.[21]

The romantic perspective of course is that she took the vow

because she deeply loved her husband and had come to a decision that she did not want to marry anyone else. This may well have been the case. But there is also a hypothesis that perhaps this vow may have either been a condition of Henry's grant to her, or a condition Katherine placed upon herself to keep her lands and property safe. As the daughter of a Yorkist King, as much as Henry had a real regard for her, he may not have felt the same about any future man that she may have chosen to marry. There is no proof that he asked her to take the vow of chastity, but it may have been a bargaining tool that saw him grant her the estates, ultimately giving her security without the threat to himself of a new husband at some point in the future using her lineage to threaten the throne. But it may also of course have been something that Katherine decided was in her own best interests. Widows in medieval times were able to run their own estates and take care of their children but once they remarried, their power completely diminished and they once again because subservient to their husband. Having been through so much upheaval and insecurity, this was finally Katherine's chance to take control of her own destiny once and for all and she must have grabbed the opportunity with both hands, never again having to rely on anyone else for help and support.

Once William had died Katherine spent less time and court and much more of her time on her Devon estates. She remained in favour with her nephew, Henry VIII, giving and receiving gifts from him, as well as several wardships. She was also given the honour of being godmother to Princess Mary.

The failed attempts to bear a healthy child is a well-known detail of the marriage of King Henry VIII and Queen Catherine of Aragon, playing a huge part in his later divorce proceedings. Before they had Mary, the King and Queen would have two more stillborn boys and a stillborn girl, and Mary was their fifth child, born on 18th February 1515 and christened three days later on 21st February in the church of the Friars Observant in

Greenwich. The church had been decorated with embroidered hangings encrusted with jewels. As well as Katherine, Mary also had the Duchess of Norfolk and Cardinal Wolsey as her other Godparents, and Katherine's son, Henry, carried the basin. The infant Mary was carried into the church by the Countess of Surrey under a gold canopy, assisted by the Dukes of Norfolk and Suffolk.[22]

As a femme sole, Katherine was now able to make a comfortable life for herself in Devon, and it seems she became a well-liked and respected member of the community. Her main residence was Tiverton Castle, which today is a privately owned house which the owners open up to the public. In an inventory taken in 1538 after the death of her eldest son, the castle is described as a mansion, moated, walled and embattled, with houses, offices and lodgings 'well-kept and repaired' with fair gardens and two parks.[23] It was originally built as a motte and bailey castle in 1106 by the de Redvers family, the first Norman Earls of Devon. As the centuries moved on, the castle was altered and enlarged and exhibits today all periods of architecture from medieval to modern, along with beautiful walled gardens.[24]

Other properties that belonged to Katherine that she would visit and stay in included Columbjohn Mansion House. The 1538 inventory recorded this as 'a fair house with diverse lodgings, well-kept'. The mansion house is first mentioned in the Domesday Book as Colump Johan, which translated literally means 'manor of John by the Culm river' and is named after Johannes de Culum who owned the manor in 1234. Nothing remains today apart from earthworks in a field and the remains of the stone arch of the gatehouse across the entrance to the field.

Colecomb Castle was another of Katherine's favoured properties. Built by the Earls of Devon in the time of Edward I, the 1538 inventory describes this as 'a fair large house with divers lodgings, well-kept, set standing within the park'. Katherine's son, Henry, rebuilt the house to a grander scale but when he was attainted in 1538 it became forfeit to the crown and left to ruin. It was later given back to his son, Edward Courtenay, by Mary I and after him came into the possession of William de la Pole (in the mid to late 17th century) who lived there for a while before allowing it to go into ruin once more. The house is now lost, although its image can be seen in two watercolours painted by the Reverend John Swete in 1795 who made two drawings of the ruins. The site is now occupied by a farm and farm buildings.[25]

But it was Tiverton that was her chief residence and for over fifteen years she lived here in relative peace and comfort, keeping in touch with her friends and family in London by letter and perhaps travelling to London and the court for special occasions. Household accounts that have survived from the period 1522-23 and 1523-24 detail payments to messengers for taking correspondence to the King and Cardinal Wolsey. She used for her title and seal 'the excellent Princess Katherine, Countess of Devon, daughter, sister and aunt of Kings' and in official documents, signed herself Katherine Devonshire.

She also paid a servant who took four horses to her daughter in London and remembered her husband William by paying for a mass on the anniversary of his death. A London Chandler was likewise paid for a year's supply of wax for Lord William's tomb.

Katherine ran her own estates with network of stewards and servants; some of her properties were administered for her by a bailiff, and some paid rent directly to her. Her influence was felt throughout the local area, an example of which can be found on a rood screen in Kenn church, which contains a panel to Saint Bridget and is the only known surviving example of a depiction of the Bridget cult in the south-west. The Courtenays presented to Kenn church and before its restoration in the nineteenth century the Courtenay arms were reportedly seen by antiquarians in the east window of the chancel and in a window in the south aisle. It is not believed that Katherine paid for the screen but the presence of Saint Bridget on one of the panels does suggest her influence, particularly because of her family connection to Saint Bridget, the saint whose name her younger sister bore. Katherine did visit the church at Kenn as she presented the new rector, Thomas Mitchell, in 1517. She certainly had a reputation in the parish for her generosity in the giving of alms and was a patron of several religious orders, inviting their members to come and preach at Columbjohn.[26] The rood screen can still be seen today in St Andrew's church in Kenn. During the reformation, many rood screens were renamed chancel screens but were often defaced or destroyed in an attempt to remove the images of saints and catholic idolatry. Amazingly the Kenn screen survived and it was renovated to its former glory in the nineteenth century.

The two years of household accounts that survive from Katherine's time at Tiverton give us a real glimpse into Katherine's life there. Over the period of a year, for instance, food consumed by Katherine and her household included forty-nine oxen, one bull, four hundred and ninety-nine sheep, two hundred and ninety-two dry hakes, two thousand, six hundred and forty-five buckhorn (dried fish), two tuns of cider, three and a half butts of Rhenish wine and Malmsey wine, cloves, cinnamon, ginger, saffron, licorice, comfits, rice and sugar candies. The household also bought soap, wax tallow candles, rushes, and horse feed oats. The accounts also detail payments for the materials for her clothes, showing purchases of various types of velvet, satin, linen and fine Holland cloth, shoes, gloves and hose.

Gifts that she gave and received are also in the accounts; the Abbot of Ford sent her a boar and two swans on 21st December one year and the Bishop of Exeter sent a red deer and one of her tenants sent her a lamb.

What we can also glean from these records is her generosity to staff. Philippa, her maid, upon her marriage received £6 13s 4d and Katherine also covered the cost of velvet for her wedding dress and kirtle, the cost of making the outfit and the cost of the wedding. 'Andrew of the kitchen' had garments made for him and her fools, Dick, Mug and Kit were well provided for as she paid for the mending and washing of their clothes. In her Will of 2nd May 1527 she made provision for her servants to be provided for for a year after her death. For the Christmas festivities, she bought a 'gallon of honey, apples and pears bought against Christmas'. Players who performed before the Countess on New Years' Eve and New Years' day were paid 13s 4d. Payments for the King and Queen's New Year gifts are listed as well as a gift to her son of two buckles, two pendants, six studs, six oiletts, six aglets (a metal tube wrapped around a shoelace) and gold and enamel garters.

William and Katherine's two surviving children, Henry and Margaret became very much involved in Henry VIII's court. There is a tale, however, that Margaret died at Colecomb Castle at a young age, after choking on a fish bone. The legend stems from an effigy of a young, almost childlike woman that can still be seen today in the parish church of Colyton. The figure is in a niche in the north wall and is of a young girl wearing a coronet with angels by her head, and a dog at her feet. The aisle where the monument is placed is called Choke-bone aisle to this day and for a long time the figure itself was known as 'little choke-a-bone'. A nineteenth century brass tablet above the effigy was inscribed: *'Margaret, daughter of William Courtenay Earl of Devon and the Princess Katharine youngest daughter of Edward IVth King of England, died at Colcombe choked by a fish-bone AD MDXII and was buried under the window in the north transept of this church'.*

That the effigy doesn't belong to Margaret Courtenay is now known because for one thing Margaret was in attendance on Princess Mary on 2nd July 1520 at Richmond.[27] She is also known to have married Henry Somerset, the eldest son of Charles Somerset, 1st Earl of Worcester and his wife Elizabeth Herbert. Elizabeth Herbert was the daughter of Katherine's aunt, Mary Woodville, so a dispensation was required for Margaret's marriage, which took place in 1514. It is now believed that the effigy is in memory of Margaret Beaufort, the wife of Thomas 5th Earl of Devon, who lived over one hundred years earlier, or one of their daughters.[28] Margaret Courtenay died before Katherine, sometime before 1527 when her husband remarried. Their son Henry, who inherited the title Earl of Devonshire upon the death of his father, was also subsequently created Marquis of Exeter by Henry VIII in 1521, on the same day that the King's bastard son, Henry Fitzroy (by his mistress, Elizabeth (Bessie) Blount) was created Earl of Somerset and Duke of Richmond. He was very much involved in life at court, spending his time among the main group of courtiers which included Charles Brandon and William Carey, husband of Mary Boleyn. William Carey was born around 1500 so was of a similar age to Henry. His father had died when he was young and his wardship and family connections with Devon suggest that there is every chance that he and Henry crossed paths in their younger years. Henry Courtenay properly entered court life in 1514, having been selected to attend the King's sister, Mary Tudor, at the French court after her marriage to the French King Louis XII. After her return to England, Henry returned to Henry VIII's court and was often seen in the company of William Carey, and it may even have been Henry who secured a place at court for William. On 4th February 1520, William Carey married Mary Boleyn and it is highly likely that Henry would have attended the wedding celebrations.[29]

Henry's star was on the rise and by 1521 he was one of only two noblemen serving in the privy chamber, which gave him daily personal access to the King. His first wife, Elizabeth Lister, whom he had married in 1515 had died in 1519 and Henry remarried that same year to a lady called Gertrude Blount, daughter of the Queen's chamberlain, William Blount and who held the position of lady in waiting to Catherine of Aragon. Gertrude would subsequently become a lifelong friend of the Queen's and her daughter Mary.

The King and Queen's marriage and accession to the throne had begun with a huge optimism for the future. The pair had been very much in love and Catherine would prove her devotion to her husband throughout the rest of her life. Henry had taken mistresses, and in that respect was no different from many other rulers and had even fathered children by them. Certainly, he had born a son with Bessie Blount and it was rumoured that at least one of Mary Boleyn's children had been Henry's. But Catherine had suffered numerous miscarriages and stillbirths in her efforts to give the King a male heir and it was this, coupled with the arrival at court in the early 1520s of Mary's now much more famous sister, Anne Boleyn, that eventually led to the downfall of their marriage. In the mid-1520s rumours began circulating that Henry planned to divorce Queen Catherine to marry Anne. It was reported by Cardinal Jean du Bellay in May 1529 that the Queen had the support of the majority of women living in England at the time: 'If the matter were to be decided by women, he (Henry VIII) would lose the battle, for they did not fail to encourage the Queen at her entrance and departure by their cries, telling her to care for nothing, and other such words'. Gertrude was one of those women who offered their full support to the Queen. At court loyalties were being tested as courtiers had to decide whose side they were on, the much-loved Queen Catherine or Henry's new paramour who it seemed more likely as each day passed that she may one day be their new Queen. For Henry and William, this may have tested their friendship as William's connections to the Boleyns were not in line with Henry and his wife, who steadfastly supported Catherine. Even after Catherine's banishment from court Gertrude continued to correspond with her, against the wishes of the King and this bought the Exeters under his suspicion. Henry Courtenay was about to discover that his closeness in kin to Henry would not necessarily save him. In his 'great matter', Henry required absolute loyalty and no matter who you were, you were either with him or against him.

On the surface, the Exeters continued to appear to support Henry's moves to divorce his wife, but in secret Gertrude had pledged her allegiance to Catherine and her daughter Mary. In 1532 Henry forbade both William and Gertrude from visiting either woman. For a while they walked a fine line, balancing their loyalty to King Henry and Catherine, and in this they must have been convincing enough as in 1533 Gertrude was asked to stand as godmother to Anne Boleyn's first child with the King, Princess Elizabeth. As the 1530s progressed it looked like the Exeters had survived a difficult period for them at court. King Henry was becoming disenchanted with the woman whom he had moved heaven and earth for in order to marry and Anne Boleyn's time as Queen was running out. Gertrude renewed her show of support for Catherine, acting as the chief source of information for the Spanish Ambassador, Eustace Chapuys, Catherine of Aragon's unrelenting supporter and champion. After Catherine's death in January 1536, Chapuys wrote several letters to his master King Charles V, who was also Catherine's nephew, informing him of her death and his worry for her daughter, Mary. In one of those letters, written on 29th January, Chapuys reported that Gertrude and her husband had been informed by one of the principal persons at Court that King Henry had confided that he had been seduced into his marriage with Anne by witchcraft.[30]

By May 1536, Anne Boleyn's time as Queen had expired. She too had been unable to provide the King with a living son, and that coupled with her championing of the 'new religion' and the fact that the love of many people at court for Queen Catherine had made them instant enemies of Anne, all led to her downfall. She was arrested along with several other men, including her brother, on arguably invented charges of adultery, incest and treason. Henry Courtenay was one of the peers who sentenced her to death.

Supporters of the old religion, Henry and Gertrude had

seemingly survived the reign of Anne Boleyn. But less than two years later they finally fell out of favour with the King and followed in Anne's footsteps when they were arrested for Henry's alleged part in a supposed plot against the King known as the 'Exeter Conspiracy'. Henry, Gertrude and their twelve-year-old son Edward were imprisoned in the tower. In 1538 Henry had begun gathering evidence against the Pole family which was headed up by Margaret Pole, daughter of George Duke of Clarence. Margaret had married Richard Pole in 1487. Margaret's sons, Henry, Baron Montague, Reginald Pole who was a Cardinal and Sir Geoffrey Pole were all accused of being involved in a plot to place Henry Courtenay on the throne. Through their family lineage, all of these men, including Henry, had Yorkist connections. King Henry, who at the beginning of his reign had shown tolerance and trust in his Yorkist kin, was now persuaded, some say erroneously by Cromwell, that a threat now existed. Henry was tried and executed for his part in the supposed plot on 9th December 1538. Margaret Pole herself was imprisoned and in arguably one of the harshest acts of Henry's reign, the old lady was executed on 27th May 1541 aged 67, in a botched execution that took several attempts to remove her head from her body. Her sons were also either executed or declared outlaws.

As for Henry's wife and son, Gertrude remained in prison until 1541. She then lived in retirement until 1553 before returning to court to serve Mary I as one of her ladies. She died in 1558. Edward was released by Mary I in 1553, aged twenty-seven years old, and she restored him to the Earldom of Devon. There was talk of his suitability as an English husband for Mary, but she never really considered him an option. Not learning from past mistakes, he became drawn into a plot known as Wyatt's rebellion, which was allegedly a plot for Edward to marry Mary's sister Elizabeth, before removing Mary from the throne and ruling in her place. However, in January 1554, he abandoned his co-conspirators and confessed his part in the scheme and was promptly dispatched back to the tower. He was released once more in 1555 and sent into exile in Europe. Arriving in Venice he came under suspicion of being involved in a second plot to put Elizabeth on the throne and marry her. Agents of Prince Phillip, Mary's husband, were dispatched to assassinate him. He died in Padua in 1556, reportedly from a fever but there is every chance he was poisoned. After his death, the Earldom of Devon went into abeyance until the 1830s.

Katherine, on her estates far away from London, would almost certainly have had an opinion on the goings-on at court but that opinion of course was never recorded. Staunchly catholic as she had been brought up, she would likely have received news of her nephew's intentions to divorce Catherine with some dismay; she would have known and met Catherine of Aragon on more than one occasion. Thankfully she did not live long enough to witness the arrest and execution of her son. As the King removed the threat of any remaining Yorkists, you cannot help but wonder whether his deep admiration and regard for Katherine would have been enough to save her had she still been living, or whether she too would eventually have fallen under his suspicion. But as it was, she did not even live long enough to see Anne Boleyn finally usurp her rival to become Henry's second wife, as on 15th November 1527, at 3pm in the afternoon, she died at her home in Tiverton. She was forty-eight years old. Her body was embalmed, cered, leaded and covered with a pall of black velvet, with a cross of white satin. Upon that was placed another pall of cloth of gold with a white cross of silver tissue garnished with six escutcheons of her arms. Katherine's body was attended day and night until Monday 21st December, when mourners wearing black hoods and gowns and carrying banners depicting the saints, escorted her body to Tiverton parish church under a canopy of black velvet. The coffin was placed under a richly decorated canopy, which was guarded all night by attendants. The mourning party then returned to Tiverton Castle for a meal.[31]

At 7am the next morning, the mourners returned to the church where a requiem mass was sung by the Abbot of Montacute, who was supported by choristers from the nearby city of Exeter. In honour of his aunt, the King sent one of his chaplains to deliver the sermon. Her Chief mourner was Lady Carew, who was assisted by Sir Piers Edgecombe. After the service, her body was buried in a vault in the Courtenay chapel on the north side of the church (probably near the site of the present vestry). Her funeral was attended by five hundred mourners including the Mayor of Exeter and City Alderman and was a testament to her popularity. After her death, eight thousand poor people were paid two pence each on the condition they prayed for her soul. In her memory, her son Henry had a tomb erected, of which there is no longer any trace; it was very likely a casualty of the Civil War.[32]

Katherine was still living when Thomas More was writing his *History of King Richard III* between 1513 and 1518, and his description of her is a perfect summing up of her life. He tells us Katherine was 'long time tossed in either fortune, sometimes in wealth, oft in adversity, at the last – if this be the last, for yet she liveth – is by the benignity of her nephew King Henry the Eighth in very prosperous estate and worthy her birth and virtue'. She did not live long enough to see the outcome of her nephew's 'great matter' that brought about not only his divorce but also radical changes to the religion that Katherine would have held so dearly. And she managed to live out her final years in peace and security and also, one hopes, she managed to find happiness. After all the adversity she experienced in her early life, this Princess of York may not have ended up as Queen of Spain as was originally intended for her by her father, but she managed to obtain for herself her own little kingdom where she could reign as Duchess of Devon.

Chapter Seven

Bridget of York

1480-1507

Bridget, which, representing the virtue of whose name she bare, professed and observed a religious life in Dartford, a house of close nuns.

Thomas More

Princess Bridget of York made her entrance into the world on 10th November 1480; unbeknownst to the King and Queen, she was to be their last child. She was born at Eltham Palace in London, just like her sister Katherine had been a little over fourteen months earlier. It is highly probable that her name was inspired by her paternal grandmother's devotion to Saint Birgitta. Birgitta Birgersdotter was born in Sweden into a powerful and noble family during the winter of 1302/3, and became known for her charity works, in particular the work she undertook assisting unmarried mothers and their children. From childhood, Birgitta began experiencing visions, but most of them occurred from the 1340s onwards; during her lifetime she claimed to have experienced around seven hundred of these revelations. After the death of her husband, she became the founder of the Brigettines nuns and monks, dying herself in 1373. Just eighteen years later, she was canonised by Pope Boniface IX, a remarkably short period after her death for her to have been awarded this recognition. From the end of the fourteenth century until well into the sixteenth, her visions proved highly influential in the devotional life of women. Bridget's grandmother, Cecily Neville, was herself an extremely pious woman, retreating as she did later in life to her castle in Berkhamsted, where she lived the life of a vowess. She certainly owned a copy of 'The Revelacions of Saint Burgitte' as she left it her Will to another of her granddaughters, Anne de la Pole, Prioress of Syon Abbey[1] and she purportedly chose the 'The Revelations' as one of the texts that would be read to her and discussed at mealtimes.[2]

At a time when infant deaths were high, it was usual for the baby to be baptised as soon as possible after birth. So it was that just twenty-four hours later, on St Martin's Day, the young princess Bridget was christened at the chapel of Eltham by the Bishop of Chichester. Details of the occasion survive and were published in 'The Gentleman's Magazine' in 1831.[3] As was the custom, her mother would not have been in attendance, the Queen would still have been lying-in after the travails of childbirth and would not emerge into public life again until after she had been churched, which would take place approximately forty to sixty days later, depending on the difficulty of the birth.

The churching ceremony marked the women's re-emergence into society and during a time when childbirth was a dangerous undertaking, churching was also a celebration of the mother's survival. For a high-ranking woman such as the Queen, it also marked her return to her duties. Elizabeth Woodville's first churching ceremony, after the birth of Princess Elizabeth, was witnessed by a visitor to the court, Gabriel Tetzel, and he left a detailed account of the occasion. The Queen was helped to rise from her bed by her ladies, who also assisted her in dressing, before she proceeded to chapel accompanied by a whole host of priests, her ladies and 'a great company of trumpeters, pipers and players of stringed instruments'. After them came the King's choir, and a huge number of heralds and knights. Elizabeth walked under a canopy, accompanied by two Dukes. Once the service had been performed, a great feast followed, which lasted for three hours, and was attended by all who had been involved 'men and women, ecclesiastical and lay, each according to rank, and filled four great rooms'.[4] For women of a lower status than the Queen, the churching ceremony would have been marked by the first time a woman returned to church after giving birth and a similar period of purification. The occasion was the same, marked by some festivities, but with less pomp and ceremony.

Even without the attendance of her parents, Bridget's christening was still a family affair and a time of celebration. The honour of carrying the new-born Princess into the chapel was awarded to Margaret Beaufort, the Countess of Richmond, who was assisted by Bridget's stepbrother Thomas Grey, the Queen's son from her first marriage. Her grandmother, Cecily Neville and Bridget's eldest sister, fourteen-year-old Elizabeth of York, were godmothers at the baptismal font and one of the Queen's sisters, and therefore Bridget's aunt, Margaret (Lady Maltravers), was also honoured as godmother to the confirmation.

In the twentieth year of the reign of King Edward IV on St. Martin's Eve was born the Lady Bridget, and christened on the morning of St. Martin's Day in the Chapel of Eltham, by the Bishop of Chichester in order as ensueth:

First a hundred torches borne by knights, esquires, and other honest persons.

The Lord Maltravers, bearing the basin, having a towel about his neck.

The Earl of Northumberland bearing a taper not lit.

The Earl of Lincoln the salt.

The canopy borne by three knights and a baron.

My lady Maltravers did bear a rich crysom pinned over her left breast.

The Countess of Richmond did bear the princess.

My lord Marquess Dorset assisted her.

My lady the king's mother, and my lady Elizabeth, were godmothers at the font.

And when the said princess was christened, a squire held the basins to the gossips [the godmothers], and even by the font my

Lady Maltravers was godmother to the confirmation.

Along with the rest of her siblings, Bridget would have spent the first two years of her life safely ensconced in the royal nursery, under the care of the household staff. The mistress of the royal nursery was Dame Elizabeth Darcy, who was rewarded by Edward IV for her services to the royal family with the grant of an annual tun of wine.[5] Elizabeth Darcy, it seemed, became a firm favourite of the royal household, as she was also appointed to oversee the nursery at the later court of Henry VII and Elizabeth of York. Elizabeth must have had fond memories of her from her childhood and keen to give her own children the same love and care that she had received. The nursery would have often been peripatetic, traveling alongside the court, but much of Bridget's first two years would likely have been spent at Eltham, which had become a favoured residence of her parents in the later years of their reign. Edward had spent much time and money turning Eltham into a grand palace and home for his family and it was he who built the magnificent grand hall that still survives today.

As well as Dame Darcy, the nursery would have consisted of several staff including a wet nurse, who would have fed the baby Bridget until she was weaned, and several rockers, employed to rock the cradle. A rocker was considered a serious and responsible position and at the later Tudor court of Henry VII and Elizabeth of York, employment as a rocker in the royal nursery could earn you as much as ten marks a year, as detailed in a letter from Henry VII to the treasurer and chamberlains of the exchequer, instructing them to pay the arrears of wages to Lady Darcy 'Lady Maistres' and 'five markes sterlinges unto oure welbeloved Agnes Butler and Emly Hobbes, rockers of our said son......their wages of the half yere.[6]

But just over two years later, life at the Yorkist court ended abruptly when her father passed away unexpectedly in April 1483. As the youngest York girl, it is likely that as an adult

Bridget would have had no recollections at all of those blessed first few years in the bosom of her family. She would also have had very few, if any, memories of her father; she was just two and a half years old when he died. Nor would she remember the flight into sanctuary made by her mother and siblings, or if she did it would only be amongst the faded shadows of childhood memories. An entry in the Privy Purse expenses of Richard of York indicates that Bridget may have been poorly around this time. The entry, dated between 9th April 1483 and 2nd February 1484, details 'To the Lady Brygitt, one of the daughters of K. Edward IIIIth, being sick in the said wardrobe for to have for her use at that time two long pillows of fustian, stuffed with down, and two pillow beres of Holland Cloth unto them'.[7] Perhaps these items were delivered to the Queen in sanctuary to make her youngest child more comfortable during her illness, or perhaps Bridget was nursed for a short time in the apartments that housed the royal wardrobe, before joining her mother in sanctuary when she was recovered.

Fortunately, blessed by her youth, Bridget would also escape the trauma of losing both her brothers, and although she may have grown up with a sadness at their loss, and that of her father, she was cushioned from the reality of events as they happened by her young age. Blissfully ignorant of the misfortune that had befallen her family, she would no doubt have adapted quickly to her new living arrangements, as resilient toddlers do.

Ten months later, on 1st March 1484, the York princesses left the sanctuary confines after Elizabeth Woodville struck an agreement with Richard III that her girls would come to no harm. Initially they were released into the care of the King and Queen, probably entering the household of Queen Anne Neville at Westminster, the only place suitable for young unmarried girls at court. When Elizabeth Woodville left the abbey precincts a short time later, she was entrusted into the keeping of Sir John Nesfield, and housed at one of his properties, most likely at

Hertford Castle or Heytesbury manor. Although it is not known for certain, it is likely that her daughters were sent to join her. Their location over the next year is unknown. The princesses were returned to court in the winter of 1484 to spend Christmas at Westminster, once again in the household of Anne Neville and Bridget may have accompanied her elder sisters, or as the youngest, and still only four years old, may have remained with her mother. If she did spend Christmas at Westminster with her elder sisters, she would, without doubt, have been returned once more into the care of her mother once the festivities were over. And there she would have remained, until after Richard's defeat at the Battle of Bosworth in August 1485, when she relocated with her mother and sisters to the apartments reserved for them at Coldharbour Place in London, to await the marriage of her eldest sister to Henry Tudor, which took place in early 1486. With her eldest daughter now Queen, Elizabeth Woodville, reinstated as dowager Queen, obtained the lease of Chenygates in the precincts of Westminster. Still only at the tender age of five and a half, Bridget would possibly have accompanied her there for a while or may have resided at court with her other siblings.

For the next few years Bridget may hopefully have been able to find some normality and been able to experience something akin to a secure and relatively happy period of her childhood. With her sister as Queen, there would have been court occasions for her to enjoy, as well as being able to spend time with her mother and sisters. However, in 1490, Bridget's life was to change again when her mother chose to retire from the court completely to live out the rest of her life in the relative peace and quiet of Bermondsey Abbey. A young Bridget, who was just ten years old, was placed into the care of the Nuns at Dartford Priory.

This may seem to us today like an unusual decision to make on behalf of a child who was still so young, but it was not unusual for noble families to dedicate one of their children to the church and it may have been that this had been planned for Bridget since she was born. If that was indeed the case, Bridget would be the only one out of all of Edward and Elizabeth's children whose life had gone exactly as they had planned for her. Her father, Edward IV, had showed a great attachment to the priory, which was the sole order of Dominican nuns in England. On 20th November 1461, just a few months after becoming King, he confirmed a past royal grant to them.[8]

Initially Bridget would just have been a ward at the priory. Constitutions stated that very young girls should not be received into monasteries, and they certainly did not allow profession before thirteen years of age.[9] The original plan may have been to send Bridget there once she had reached the age of thirteen, but perhaps circumstances as they were, dictated that she should be sent there earlier than intended. Dartford was known for its educational work amongst children and young women from well to do families, and the nunnery had a notable reputation as a place of learning, so was an ideal choice for a young princess. In 1481, Sister Jane Fitzh'er (sic) had requested that they be allowed to have a teacher of grammar and Latin, who might enter the common parlour, which was a room or rooms within the nunnery where the nuns would congregate as a group. This request was granted by the Master-General, and a teacher was sought who instructed not only the nuns and novices, but also the daughters of noble families who had been sent to Dartford for their education. There is also some evidence that boys may even have been taught in the nunnery.[10]

The Prioress at the time of Bridget's admittance to Dartford was Elizabeth Cressner, who had become Prioress in 1488 and oversaw her community for the next fifty years. Founded by Edward III in the 1340s, the Dominican nuns who inhabited the priory were also known as 'Sisters of the Order of St. Augustine'.

Life at the priory would have been hard, particularly for a young child. The nuns dressed simply, in a black mantle and veil over a white habit tied with a leather belt. The habit was made of unfinished and undyed wool, expressing penance, purity and poverty. Meals at the priory were scanty, often consisting of only bread and water, and the nuns would have observed several fast days. All meals would be taken in silence, perhaps whilst listening to an educational or devotional reading. Time that was not spent in prayer and contemplation, would have been spent sewing or undertaking embroidery, again in silence. At certain times it would have been permissible for one of them to read aloud from scriptures whilst the others sewed.[11]

At some time after her thirteenth birthday, Bridget would have taken the veil. She was supported at the priory by her sister, Queen Elizabeth, who made payments to the Prioress of Dartford for her maintenance out of her privy purse. The privy purse accounts show that she contributed twenty marks a year towards her upkeep. On 6th July 1502 a payment was made by the Queen to the Abbess of Dartford for £3 6s 8d for her keep and on 28th September 1502, a messenger was paid 2s 'for his costes riding from Windsore to Dartford to my lady Brigget by the space of twoo days at 2d'.[12]

Although much of her life was spent within the priory walls, Brigitte was not totally confined there and was able to leave in exceptional circumstances, such as when her mother became sick in early 1492. Bridget visited her mother at Bermondsey during this period and nursed her. She also attended her funeral in June 1492.

The funeral of the Dowager Queen was a humble affair for a woman who had been Queen, as directed in Elizabeth's Will where she had requested to be buried at Windsor with her husband 'without pompes entring or costlie expensis donne thereabought'. She died on Friday 8th June and on Sunday 10th June was taken by river to Windsor and buried immediately on arrival. Over the following days mourners arrived, and services were held. Bridget and two of her sisters arrived on the

Tuesday: 'On the Tewsday theder came by water iiij of kynges Edwardes doughters and heirs, that is to say the Lady Anne, the Lady Katherine, the Lady Bregett accompeygned with the Lady Marquys of Dorsett, the Duc of Buckyngham daughter of nyce of the fore said qwene'.[13] Her other two living sisters, Cecily and Elizabeth, were both indisposed and unable to attend. The Lady Marquess of Dorset was their sister-in-law, Cecily, married to their half-brother, Thomas and the final lady in their party was their cousin Elizabeth Buckingham, the daughter of Katherine Woodville, sister to the Queen.

As well as her mother and sister, she was hopefully able to maintain contact with other members of her family, even if only by letter. Her grandmother, Cecily, certainly remembered her and bequeathed three books to her in her Will dated April 1st, and proved 27th August 1495 'the boke of Legenda Aurea in velem, a boke of the life of Saint Kateryn of Sene, a boke of Saint Matilde'.[14]

Bridget, sadly, did not live a long life. Many sources give her death as 1517, but Thomas More writing in 1513, states that out of Elizabeth's sisters, Katherine, was still living, which suggests that the others, including Bridget, had died by then. An entry in The Chamber Books of Henry VII seem to confirm she died in or just before 1507 and was buried in the choir at Dartford.[15] She would have been around twenty-seven years of age.

1507. Itm. for a marbulstone bought to ley upon my lady brygett within the quere of dartford 46s 8d.

She thankfully did not survive to see the closure of the priory during the reign of her nephew, Henry VIII, which took place sometime after 1st April, 1539, when the bishop of Dover begged Thomas Cromwell to let him 'have the receiving' of Dartford.[16] The dissolution of the monasteries, orchestrated by Henry VIII and his chief minister, Cromwell, changed the face of religion in England forever and ended a way of life for the monks and nuns who inhabited these institutions and who suddenly found themselves homeless. The Prioress, Elizabeth, was still in charge in 1539 at a great old age and was pensioned off with a sum of 100 marks. Bridget's final resting place disappeared along with the destruction of the rest of the priory.

Looking back on Bridget's life, it can be said she led a relatively simple and peaceful life, the tumultuous years occurring when she was too young for them to have too much of an impact. But the story of her life cannot be ended without a brief mention of the whiff of a scandal that has been attributed to her. The rumour concerns a young girl called Agnes of Eltham, who by all accounts was born in or around 1498 and who some believe may be Bridget's daughter. Agnes is mentioned in several sources, including 'Elizabeth of York' by Alison Weir and 'Henry VII, the Maligned Tudor King' by Terry Breverton. That Agnes existed and lived at the priory is undisputed, but according to the tale, the child was also supported by Queen Elizabeth, who made payments towards her upkeep from the privy purse, although conclusive proof of this cannot be found. It is also said that Agnes left the priory around 1514, marrying a gentleman called Adam Langstroth, the head of a landed gentry family in Yorkshire. This is not unusual in itself, but the fact that she apparently left Dartford with a considerable dowry adds fuel to the story that she was supported by someone with money and influence.

No contemporary sources have mentioned Bridget having a child and the story is probably little more than coincidence and rumour. Queen Elizabeth may well have met young Agnes on a visit to the priory and felt an attachment to the child, enough to make her decide to contribute towards her upkeep. However, it is not beyond the realms of possibility of course that Bridget did bear a child, who was taken in by the nuns and supported in her upkeep by the King and Queen, who also arranged a good marriage for her. Particularly if boys were indeed educated at the priory, there is a chance that a teenage Bridget met and entered into an illicit relationship with a young man that through love, desire or possibly simple ignorance, resulted in a pregnancy that had to be hushed up. It is tempting to want to add a dangerous liaison, and even a brief spell of love and happiness into her otherwise seemingly sedate existence, even though in reality it is more likely that Agnes and Bridget were nothing more than members of the same institution.

John Speed in the seventeenth century wrote that Bridget of York 'spent her life in holy contemplation unto the day of her death'.[17] Amidst the troubled years of the Wars of the Roses, a peaceful existence is something many of her contemporaries would have yearned for. Dedicating her life to the service of others and the service of God, her namesake, Saint Birgitta, would have surely approved.

The End of an Era

As a collective, the lives of the Princesses of York spanned seven decades and the rule of five English Kings. Out of the seven girls, Mary and Margaret did not live long lives, and during the few years they were on earth, they led a relatively stable existence. But their five sisters, Elizabeth, Cecily, Anne, Katherine and Bridget had a much more eventful time, their early childhoods spent in the luxury of their parent's court, before their lives were thrown into chaos during the tumultuous years of 1483-5, and then finding themselves having to navigate and find their place in the new Tudor regime.

The people of England had little choice but to adapt to whichever ruler was on the throne. From the death of the highly competent and hugely popular Edward IV, through the disappearance of the rightful new King Edward V, the usurpation years of Richard III and then into the new years of the Tudor dynasty, noblemen and commoners alike watched events unfold and adapted according to their position and their beliefs. But for the Princesses of York, the events were personal. As the four-hundred-year reign of the Plantagenet Kings came to an end, they lost their father, their brothers, their uncles and their male cousins, often by the hands of their own family members. Ultimately it was the Plantagenet women who were the greatest survivors, left behind to mourn their male relatives and to adjust to a new and unpredicted world.

From their father, Edward IV, his daughters inherited his popularity and loyalty of the common people. This was particularly true in Elizabeth's case, who was very much the lynch pin in the fledgling Tudor court; her presence made Henry Tudor's acceptance onto the throne all the much easier. From their mother, they inherited her strikingly good looks. All of the York girls and Cecily in particular were said to be remarkably attractive.

Sadly, none of them proved as fertile as their mother who had given birth to twelve children, or their grandmother, Jacquetta Woodville who had given birth to at least fifteen children. Both Cecily and Anne would suffer the trauma of multiple childhood deaths and Katherine only had three children that we know of. Elizabeth would fare the best, giving birth at least eight times, although only three of them would reach adulthood (four if you count Prince Arthur, who died as a young adult). Katherine's descendants would of course die out with the death of her grandson, Edward in 1556 and it was only Elizabeth whose bloodline would continue. Her descendants would also continue to rule England, although not through the House of Tudor. Her son, Henry VIII and her three grandchildren, Mary I, Edward VI and Elizabeth I would all take their turn on the throne, but the House of Tudor would end with the death of Elizabeth I. It was through her daughter, Margaret, who married the Scots King James IV that the Plantagenet blood would continue. Margaret was grandmother to Mary Queen of Scots and thus the great-grandmother of James VI, who of course later became James I of England after Queen Elizabeth I died childless.

Out of the five surviving sisters, Elizabeth, Cecily, Anne, Katherine and Bridget, the two elder York girls would likely recall their early lives under Plantagenet rule – they were seventeen and fourteen when their father died. But for the younger York Princesses, Anne, Katherine and Bridget, who were eight, four and two at the death of their father, they would likely have had few if any memories at all of their early life; they spent a larger part of their young lives growing up at the court of their sister, Elizabeth.

Katherine was the last surviving York Princess and by the time of her death in 1529, the courts and daily life of the Plantagenet Kings were becoming a distant memory. A few years after her death, her nephew King Henry would divorce

Catherine of Aragon to marry Anne Boleyn, break from Rome and declare himself Head of the Church of England. The age of chivalric knights and crusades was passing and the face of religion in England was changing dramatically as monasteries were closed down and the 'new religion' began to flourish. The biggest religious change in English history was underway, as images of saints and shrines were destroyed, and 'popish' worship was forbidden. Over time the reliance on saints and holy pilgrimages would fall into abeyance as the country slowly became a Protestant nation. At the same time learning and the arts began to flourish, the introduction of the printing press made books and pamphlets more easily accessible for the common people and less than thirty years after Katherine's death, England would see its first female ruler in the shape of her great niece, Mary Tudor.

Had their destiny been as their father had originally wished for them, their adult lives would have been spent in foreign realms – Elizabeth in France, Cecily in Scotland, Anne in Austria and Katherine in Spain. Bridget was the exception; she it seems had been destined for the service of God at an early age and her life did mirror that which had been planned for her.

But instead they all lived a very different life that was expected of them, in part due to their father's untimely death, but more specifically due to the usurpation of their brother's throne by their uncle Richard. With a single action, the course of their future changed dramatically, the consequences of which led them to remain in England and become part of our rich tapestry of history.

References

The First Reign of Edward IV

1. Jones, Dan. *The Hollow Crown: The Wars of The Roses and the Rise of the Tudors*, Faber & Faber, 2015.
2. Licence, Amy. *Edward IV and Elizabeth Woodville*, Amberley Publishing, 2016.
3. Steward, Desmond. *The Wars of the Roses*. Robinson, 2007.
4. Jones, Dan. *The Hollow Crown: The Wars of The Roses and the Rise of the Tudors*, Faber & Faber, 2015.

Chapter One

1. Strickland, Agnes. *Memoirs of the Queens of Henry VIII and of his mother, Elizabeth of York*, Blanchard and Lea, 1853.
2. Weir, Alison. *Elizabeth of York: The First Tudor Queen*, Vintage, 2014.
3. Gairdner James (ed.). *Project Gutenberg online: The Paston Letters, A.D. 1422-1509, Vol. V.*
4. Baldwin, *Elizabeth Woodville, Mother of the Princes in the Tower*, David Sutton Publishing, 2002.
5. Sutton, Anne F. and Visser-Fuchs, Livia. *The Prophecy of G.* The Ricardian, Sept 1990.
6. Jones, Dan. *The Hollow Crown: The Wars of The Roses and the Rise of the Tudors*, Faber & Faber, 2015.
7. Jones, Dan. *The Hollow Crown: The Wars of The Roses and the Rise of the Tudors*, Faber & Faber, 2015.
8. Croyland Chronicle.
9. Okerlund, A. *Elizabeth of York*, Palgrave Macmillan, 2009.
10. Vergil, Polydore (Sir Henry Ellis K.H. ed). *Three Books of Polydore Vergil's English History: Comprising the Reigns of Henry VI, Edward IV and Richard III*. Camden Society, 1844.
11. Weir, Alison. *Elizabeth of York: The First Tudor Queen*, Vintage, 2014.

12. Strickland, Agnes. *Lives of the Queens of England from the Norman Conquest*, Lea and Blanchard, 1852.

13. Strickland, Agnes. *Lives of the Queens of England from the Norman Conquest*, Lea and Blanchard, 1852.

14. Gairdner James (ed.). *Project Gutenberg online: The Paston Letters, A.D. 1422-1509, Vol. V.*

15. Leland, *Joannis Lelandi Antiquarii de rebus Britannicis Collectanea (vol. 5)*, Thomas Hearne, 1770.

16. Saint Claire Byrne, Muriel (ed.) *The Lisle Letters – an Abridgement*, University of Chicago Press, 1983.

17. Nicolas, Sir Nicholas Harris. *Privy purse expenses of Elizabeth of York; Wardrobe Accounts of Edward the Fourth. With a memoir of Elizabeth of York*, Sir Nicholas Harris. William Pickering, 1830.

18. Norton, Elizabeth. *The Lives of Tudor Women*, Head of Zeus, 2017.

19. Nicolas, Sir Nicholas Harris. *Privy purse expenses of Elizabeth of York; Wardrobe Accounts of Edward the Fourth. With a memoir of Elizabeth of York*, Sir Nicholas Harris. William Pickering, 1830.

Chapter Two

1. Green, Mary Anne Everett. *Lives of the Princesses of England from the Norman Conquest, Vol 3*, Longman, Brown, Green, Longman & Roberts, London 1857.

2. Weir, Alison. *Elizabeth of York: The First Tudor Queen*, Vintage, 2014.

3. Sutton, Anne F., Visser-Fuchs, Livia, Hammond, P.W. *The Reburial of Richard, Duke of York, 21-30 July 1476*, The Ricardian, Volume X, Dec 1994.

4. Weir, Alison. *Elizabeth of York: The First Tudor Queen*, Vintage, 2014.

5. Jones, Philomena. *Anne Mowbray*, The Ricardian, Volume V, June 1978.

6. Sutton and Visser-Fuch, *Royal Funerals of the House of York at Windsor*, Richard III Society, 2005.

7. Green, Mary Anne Everett. *Lives of the Princesses of England from the Norman Conquest, Vol 3*, Longman, Brown, Green, Longman & Roberts, London 1857.

Chapter Three

1. Licence, Amy. *Edward IV and Elizabeth Woodville: A True Romance*, Amberley Publishing, 2016.

2. Okerlund, A. *Elizabeth of York*, Palgrave Macmillan, 2009.

3. Ibid

4. Licence, Amy. *Edward IV and Elizabeth Woodville: A True Romance*, Amberley Publishing, 2016.

5. Weir, Alison. *Elizabeth of York: The First Tudor Queen*, Vintage, 2014.

6. Ibid.

7. Ibid

8. Leland, *Joannis Lelandi Antiquarii de rebus Britannicis Collectanea (Vol. 5)*, Thomas Hearne, 1770.

9. Ibid

10. Richardson, Douglas. *Magna Carta Ancestry: a study in colonial and medieval families*, Genealogical Publishing Company, 2005.

11. Nicolas, Sir Nicholas Harris. *Privy purse expenses of Elizabeth of York; Wardrobe Accounts of Edward the Fourth. With a memoir of Elizabeth of York*, Sir Nicholas Harris. William Pickering, 1830.

12. Weir, Alison. *Elizabeth of York: The First Tudor Queen*, Vintage, 2014.

13. Richardson, Douglas. *Magna Carta Ancestry: a study in colonial and medieval families*, Genealogical Publishing Company, 2005.

14. Archaeology at Bloomberg by MOLA

15. Baldwin, *Elizabeth Woodville, Mother of the Princes in the*

Tower, David Sutton Publishing, 2002.

16. Green, Mary Anne Everett. *Lives of the Princesses of England from the Norman Conquest, Vol 3*, Longman, Brown, Green, Longman & Roberts, London 1857.

17. Weir, Alison. *Elizabeth of York: The First Tudor Queen*, Vintage, 2014.

18. Nicolas, Sir Nicholas Harris. *Privy purse expenses of Elizabeth of York; Wardrobe Accounts of Edward the Fourth. With a memoir of Elizabeth of York*, Sir Nicholas Harris. William Pickering, 1830.

19. Thompson, Pishey. *The history and antiquities of Boston, and the villages of Skirbeck, Fishtoft, Freiston, Butterwick, Benington, Leverton Leake and Wrangle; comprising the hundred of Skirbeck in the country of Lincoln*, J. Noble, Boston, 1856.

20. Richardson, Douglas. *Magna Carta Ancestry: a study in colonial and medieval families*, Genealogical Publishing Company, 2005.

21. 'Parishes: Arreton', in A History of the County of Hampshire: Volume 5, ed. William Page (London, 1912), pp. 139-151. British History Online.

22. Wroe, Anne. *Perkin: A Story of Deception*, Vintage, 2004.

23. Worsley, Sir Richard. *History of the Isle Of Wight*, A. Hamilton, 1781.

24. Weir, Alison. *Elizabeth of York: The First Tudor Queen*, Vintage, 2014.

25. *The Penny Magazine of the Society for the Diffusion of Useful knowledge*, 1836. Volume 5.

Chapter Four

1. Jones, Dan. *The Hollow Crown: The Wars of The Roses and the Rise of the Tudors*, Faber & Faber, 2015.

2. Licence, Amy. *Edward IV and Elizabeth Woodville: A True Romance,* Amberley Publishing, 2016.

3. Gairdner James (ed.). *Project Gutenberg online: The Paston*

Letters, A.D. 1422-1509, Vol. V.

4. All Saints Church, Maidstone: www.maidstoneallsaints. co.uk

5. Seward, Desmond. *The Wars of the Roses,* Viking Penguin, 1995.

6. Stow, John. *A Survey of the Cities of London and Westminster, Borough of Southwark, and Parts Adjacent ... Being an Improvement of Mr. Stow's, and Other Surveys, by Adding Whatever Alterations Have Happened in the Said Cities, &c. to the Present Year,* T Read, 1735.

7. Ibid

Chapter Five

1. Green, Mary Anne Everett. *Lives of the Princesses of England from the Norman Conquest, Vol 4,* Longman, Brown, Green, Longman & Roberts, London 1857.

2. Licence, Amy. *Edward IV and Elizabeth Woodville: A True Romance,* Amberley Publishing, 2016.

3. Dean, Kristie. *On The Trail of the Yorks,* Amberley Publishing, 2016.

4. Dean, Kristie. *On The Trail of the Yorks,* Amberley Publishing, 2016.

5. *The Gentleman's Magazine.* Sylvanus Urban. 1845

6. Leland, *Joannis Lelandi Antiquarii de rebus Britannicis Collectanea,* Thomas Hearne, 1770.

7. Weir, Alison. *Elizabeth of York: The First Tudor Queen,* Vintage, 2014.

8. Sutton and Visser-Fuch, *Royal Funerals of the House of York at Windsor,* Richard III Society, 2005.

9. Nicolas, Sir Nicholas Harris. *Privy purse expenses of Elizabeth of York; Wardrobe Accounts of Edward the Fourth. With a memoir of Elizabeth of York,* Sir Nicholas Harris. William Pickering, 1830.

10. Green, Mary Anne Everett. *Lives of the Princesses of England*

from the Norman Conquest, Vol 4. Longman, Brown, Green, Longman & Roberts, London 1857.

11. *The Gentleman's Magazine.* Sylvanus Urban. 1845

12. Nicolas, Sir Nicholas Harris. *Privy purse expenses of Elizabeth of York; Wardrobe Accounts of Edward the Fourth. With a memoir of Elizabeth of York,* Sir Nicholas Harris. William Pickering, 1830.

13. Norfolk House and Old Paradise Street, in Survey of London: Volume 23, Lambeth: South Bank and Vauxhall, ed. Howard Roberts and Walter H Godfrey (London, 1951), pp. 137-140. British History Online.

14. *The Early Career of Thomas, Lord Howard, Earl of Surrey and Third Duke of Norfolk, 1474 - c. 1525* being a Thesis submitted for the Degree of Doctor of Philosophy in the University of Hull by Susan Elisabeth Vokes, B.A.

15. Heal, Felicity. *The Power of Gifts: Gift-exchange in Early Modern England,* OUP Oxford, 2014.

16. Emery, Anthony. *Greater Medieval Houses of England and Wales, 1300-1500 (volume 2),* Cambridge University Press, 2000.

17. Torlesse, Charles Martin (Vicar). *Some Account of Stoke by Nayland, Suffolk.* Harrison & Sons, London, 1877.

18. Ibid

19. www.gardenmuseum.org.uk

20. Weir, Alison. *Elizabeth of York: The First Tudor Queen,* Vintage, 2014.

21. Hall's Chronicle.

22. Weir, Alison. *Elizabeth of York: The First Tudor Queen,* Vintage, 2014.

23. Crawford, Anne. *The Career of John Howard, Duke of Norfolk. 1420-1485.* Unpublished M. Phil, thesis. University of London, 1975.

24. Houses of Cluniac monks: The priory of St Mary, Thetford, in A History of the County of Norfolk: Volume 2, ed. William

Page (London, 1906), pp. 363-369. British History Online.

25. Ashdown-Hill, John. *The Opening of the Tombs of the Dukes of Richmond and Norfolk, Framlingham, April 1841: the Account of the Reverend J.W. Darby*, Ricardian, Vol. 18, 2008.

26. Robinson, John Martin. *The Dukes of Norfolk*, Phillimore & Co. Ltd., 1995.

Chapter Six

1. Sutton and Visser-Fuch, *Royal Funerals of the House of York at Windsor*, Richard III Society, 2005.

2. *Tudor and Stuart Devon: The Common Estate and Government*: Essays presented to Joyce Younings. Todd Grey, Margery M. Rowe, Audrey M. Erskine. University of Exeter Press, 1992.

3. Ibid

4. Cleaveland, Ezra. *A Genealogical History of the Noble and Illustrious Family of Courtenay*, 1735.

5. *Tudor and Stuart Devon: The Common Estate and Government*: Essays presented to Joyce Younings. Todd Grey, Margery M. Rowe, Audrey M. Erskine. University of Exeter Press, 1992.

6. Cleaveland, Ezra. *A Genealogical History of the Noble and Illustrious Family of Courtenay*, 1735.

7. Weir, Alison. *Elizabeth of York: The First Tudor Queen*, Vintage, 2014.

8. Walter Thornbury, 'Newgate Street', in Old and New London: Volume 2 (London, 1878), pp. 427-441. British History Online.

9. *Cleaveland, Ezra. A Genealogical History of the Noble and Illustrious Family of Courtenay*, 1735.

10. 'Parishes: Havering-atte-Bower', in A History of the County of Essex: Volume 7, ed. W R Powell (London, 1978), pp. 9-17. British History Online.

11. Weir, Alison. *Elizabeth of York: The First Tudor Queen*, Vintage, 2014.

12. Nicholas, Sir Nicholas Harris. *Privy purse expenses of Elizabeth*

of York; Wardrobe Accounts of Edward the Fourth. With a memoir of Elizabeth of York, William Pickering, 1830.

13. Ibid

14. Ibid

15. Ibid

16. Weir, Alison. *Elizabeth of York: The First Tudor Queen*, Vintage, 2014.

17. Ibid

18. *Tudor and Stuart Devon: The Common Estate and Government*: Essays presented to Joyce Younings. Todd Grey, Margery M. Rowe, Audrey M. Erskine. University of Exeter Press, 1992.

19. Cleaveland, Ezra. *A Genealogical History of the Noble and Illustrious Family of Courtenay*, 1735.

20. Lipscomb, George. The History and Antiquities of the County of Buckingham, Vol 1. J. & W. Robins, 1847.

21. Nicholas, Sir Nicholas Harris. *Privy purse expenses of Elizabeth of York; Wardrobe Accounts of Edward the Fourth. With a memoir of Elizabeth of York*, William Pickering, 1830

22. Licence, Amy. *Catherine of Aragon*, Amberley Publishing, 2016.

23. *Tudor and Stuart Devon: The Common Estate and Government*: Essays presented to Joyce Younings. Todd Grey, Margery M. Rowe, Audrey M. Erskine. University of Exeter Press, 1992.

24. Tiverton Castle website: www.tivertoncastle.com

25. Dugdale, James. *The new British traveller; or, a Modern panorama of England and Wales; exhibiting an account, historical, topographical, and statistical, of this portion of the British Empire, interspersed with biographical particulars of eminent and remarkable persons*, 1819.

26. *The Medieval Mystical Tradition in England: Exeter Symposium VII*: Papers read at Charney Manor, July 2004.

27. *The Visitation of the County of Devon: Comprising the Heralds' Visitations of 1531, 1564 & 1620*, Exeter, 1895.

28. Pevsner, Nikolaus & Cherry, Bridget. *The Buildings of*

England: Devon, Penguin Books, 1989, p.280.

29. Wilkinson, Josephine. *Mary Boleyn: The true story of Henry VIII's Favourite Mistress,* Amberley Publishing, 2011.

30. 'Henry VIII: January 1536, 26-31', in Letters and Papers, Foreign and Domestic, Henry VIII, Volume 10, January-June 1536, ed. James Gairdner (London, 1887), pp. 64-81. British History Online.

31. *Tudor and Stuart Devon: The Common Estate and Government:* Essays presented to Joyce Younings. Todd Grey, Margery M. Rowe, Audrey M. Erskine. University of Exeter Press, 1992.

32. Tiverton Church website: www.stpeterstiverton.org.uk

Chapter Seven

1. Licence, Amy. *Cecily Neville: Mother of Kings,* Amberley Publishing, 2014.

2. Sahlin, Claire Lynn. *Birgitta of Sweden and the Voice of Prophecy,* Boydell Press, 2000.

3. "F.M.," "Christening of the Princess Bridget, 1480." *Gentleman's Magazine,* January 1831.

4. Licence, Amy. *Edward IV and Elizabeth Woodville: A True Romance,* Amberley Publishing, 2016.

5. Harris, *English Aristocratic Women, 1450-1550: Marriage and Family, Property and Careers,* Oxford University Press, 2002.

6. Nicolas, Sir Nicholas Harris. *Privy purse expenses of Elizabeth of York; Wardrobe Accounts of Edward the Fourth. With a memoir of Elizabeth of York,* Sir Nicholas Harris. William Pickering, 1830.

7. Ibid

8. Palmer, Rev. CFR. *Notes on the Priory of Dartford in Kent,* The Archaeological Journal, Royal Archaeological Institute, 2013.

9. Lee, Paul. Nunneries, Learning and Spirituality in Late Medieval Society. Boydell & Brewer Ltd., 2001.

10. 'Friaries: The Dominican nuns of Dartford', in A History of

the County of Kent: Volume 2, ed. William Page (London, 1926), pp. 181-190. British History Online.

11. Lee, Paul. *Nunneries, Learning and Spirituality in Late Medieval Society*, Boydell & Brewer Ltd., 2001.

12. Palmer, Rev. CFR. *Notes on the Priory of Dartford in Kent*, The Archaeological Journal, Royal Archaeological Institute, 2013.

13. Sutton and Visser-Fuch, *Royal Funerals of the House of York at Windsor*, Richard III Society, 2005.

14. Palmer, Rev. CFR. *Notes on the Priory of Dartford in Kent*, The Archaeological Journal, Royal Archaeological Institute, 2013.

15. Tudor Chamber Books Online

16. 'Friaries: The Dominican nuns of Dartford', in A History of the County of Kent: Volume 2, ed. William Page (London, 1926), pp. 181-190. British History Online.

17. Weir, Alison. *Elizabeth of York: The First Tudor Queen*, Vintage, 2014.

Select Bibliography

With the exception of Elizabeth, the York princesses are only ever part of the supporting cast in most books and never the main protagonists. But to give you a feel for the period they lived in, the following books are a recommended read.

Baldwin, David, *Elizabeth Woodville, Mother of the Princes in the Tower*, Sutton Publishing, 2002.

Dean, Kristie, *On The Trail of the Yorks*. Amberley Publishing, 2016.

Dunleavy, Brian, *The Woodville Chronicle*, Magic Flute Artworks Ltd., 2017.

Fox, Julia, *Sister Queens: Katherine of Aragon and Juana Queen of Castille*, W&N, 2012.

Gregory, Phillipa, *The Women of the Cousins War: The Real White Queen and her Rivals*, Simon & Schuster Ltd, 2013.

Gristwood, Sarah, *Blood Sisters: The Women behind the Wars of the Roses*, Harper Collins, 2013.

Grueninger, Natalie, *Discovering Tudor London: A Journey Back in Time*, The History Press, 2017.

Harris, Barbara J., *English Aristocratic Women, 1450-1550: Marriage and Family, Property and Careers*, Oxford University Press, 2002.

Hicks, Michael, *The Family of Richard III*, Amberley Publishing, 2015.

Higginbotham, Susan, *The Woodvilles*, The History Press, 2013.

Hodder, Sarah J. *The Queen's Sisters: The Lives of the Sisters of Elizabeth Woodville*, John Hunt Publishing, 2020.

Jones, Dan, *The Hollow Crown: The Wars of the Roses and the Rise of the Tudors*, Faber & Faber, 2014.

Leyser, Henrietta, *Medieval Women: A Social History of Women in England 450-1500*, W&N, 2005.

Licence, Amy, *Catherine of Aragon: An Intimate Life of Henry VII's True Wife*, Amberley Publishing, 2016.

Licence, Amy, *Edward IV and Elizabeth Woodville*, Amberley Publishing, 2016.

Licence, Amy, *Elizabeth of York – Forgotten Tudor Queen*, Amberley Publishing, 2013.

Macgibbon, David, *Elizabeth Woodville – A Life: The Real Story of the White Queen*, 2013.

Okerlund, A. *Elizabeth of York*, Palgrave Macmillan, 2009.

Sutton and Visser-Fuch, *Royal Funerals of the House of York at Windsor*, Richard III Society, 2005.

Weir, Alison, *Elizabeth of York: The First Tudor Queen*, Ballantine Books, 2014.

Weir, Alison, *Lancaster and York*, Vintage, 2009.

Wilkinson, Josephine, *Mary Boleyn: The true story of Henry VIII's Favourite Mistress*, Amberley Publishing, 2011.

CHRONOS
BOOKS

HISTORY

Chronos Books is an historical non-fiction imprint. Chronos
publishes real history for real people; bringing to life people,
places and events in an imaginative, easy-to-digest and
accessible way - histories that pass on their stories to a
generation of new readers.
If you have enjoyed this book, why not tell other readers by
posting a review on your preferred book site.

Recent bestsellers from Chronos Books are:

Lady Katherine Knollys
The Unacknowledged Daughter of King Henry VIII
Sarah-Beth Watkins
A comprehensive account of Katherine Knollys' questionable
paternity, her previously unexplored life in the Tudor court
and her intriguing relationship with Elizabeth I.
Paperback: 978-1-78279-585-8 ebook: 978-1-78279-584-1

Cromwell was Framed
Ireland 1649
Tom Reilly
Revealed: The definitive research that proves the Irish nation
owes Oliver Cromwell a huge posthumous apology for
wrongly convicting him of civilian atrocities in 1649.
Paperback: 978-1-78279-516-2 ebook: 978-1-78279-515-5

Why The CIA Killed JFK and Malcolm X
The Secret Drug Trade in Laos
John Koerner
A new groundbreaking work presenting evidence that the CIA
silenced JFK to protect its secret drug trade in Laos.
Paperback: 978-1-78279-701-2 ebook: 978-1-78279-700-5

The Disappearing Ninth Legion
A Popular History
Mark Olly
The Disappearing Ninth Legion examines hard evidence for the
foundation, development, mysterious disappearance, or possi-
ble continuation of Rome's lost Legion.
Paperback: 978-1-84694-559-5 ebook: 978-1-84694-931-9

Beaten But Not Defeated

Siegfried Moos - A German anti-Nazi who settled in Britain
Merilyn Moos
Siegi Moos, an anti-Nazi and active member of the German
Communist Party, escaped Germany in 1933 and, exiled in
Britain, sought another route to the transformation
of capitalism.
Paperback: 978-1-78279-677-0 ebook: 978-1-78279-676-3

A Schoolboy's Wartime Letters

An evacuee's life in WWII — A Personal Memoir
Geoffrey Iley
A boy writes home during WWII, revealing his own fascinating
story, full of zest for life, information and humour.
Paperback: 978-1-78279-504-9 ebook: 978-1-78279-503-2

The Life & Times of the Real Robyn Hoode

Mark Olly
A journey of discovery. The chronicles of the genuine historical
character, Robyn Hoode, and how he became one of England's
greatest legends.
Paperback: 978-1-78535-059-7 ebook: 978-1-78535-060-3

Readers of ebooks can buy or view any of these bestsellers by clicking on the live link in the title. Most titles are published in paperback and as an ebook. Paperbacks are available in traditional bookshops. Both print and ebook formats are available online.

Find more titles and sign up to our readers' newsletter at http://www.johnhuntpublishing.com/history-home

Follow us on Facebook at https://www.facebook.com/ChronosBooks

and Twitter at https://twitter.com/ChronosBooks